W9-CUP-974

COLLAGE SOURCEBOOK

QUARRY

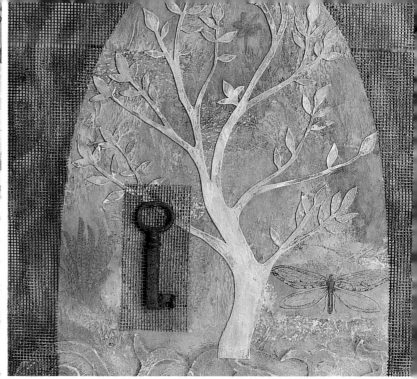

COLLAGE SOURCEBOOK

EXPLORING THE ART AND TECHNIQUES OF COLLAGE

GLOUCESTER MASSACHUSETTS

QUARRY BOOKS

© 2005 by Quarry Books

All rights reserved. No part of this book may be reproduced in any form without written permission of the copyright owners. All images in this book have been reproduced with the knowledge and prior consent of the artists concerned, and no responsibility is accepted by producer, publisher, or printer for any infringement of copyright or otherwise, arising from the contents of this publication. Every effort has been made to ensure that credits accurately comply with information supplied.

First published in the United States of America by

Quarry Books, an imprint of

Rockport Publishers, Inc.

33 Commercial Street

Gloucester, Massachusetts 01930-5089

Telephone: (978) 282-9590

Fax: (978) 283-2742

www.rockpub.com

Library of Congress Cataloging-in-Publication Data available

ISBN 1-59253-101-6

10 9 8 7 6 5 4 3 2

Layout and production: Susan Raymond

Cover Images:
top left: Helen Orth; top right: Paula Grasdal;
bottom left: Paula Grasdal; bottom right: Dominie Nash

Grateful acknowledgment is given to Jennifer Atkinson for her work from *Collage Art: A Step-by-Step Guide and Showcase* (Quarry Books 1996) on pages 8–11 and pages 15–139; and to Paula Grasdal and Holly Harrison for their work from *Collage for the Soul: Expressing Hopes and Dreams through Art* (Rockport Publishers 2003) on pages 12–14 and pages 140–261.

Printed in China

CONTENTS

INTRODUCTION

Collage had a long, vital history as a folk art before it emerged as a fine art in the twentieth century. In Europe, Asia, and the Americas, all kinds of everyday materials were transformed into mementos and decorations: pictures made of matchsticks, straw, butterfly wings, or feathers; portrait silhouettes cut carefully from paper and framed; fancy paper Valentines garnished with bits of lace and cutout papers; and pressed flower arrangements. In the early 1900s, the modernist avant-garde adopted collage as a medium, making it an integral part of the evolution of modern art. It suited the modernists' radical reinterpretation of the picture plane (they rejected one-point perspective and the attempt to portray "real space" in two-dimensional work). Collage's celebration of common materials, typically considered beneath the purposes of fine art, also appealed to them—they wished to create art that could be reproduced easily, made from readily available materials.

Collage continues to appeal to professional artists (even those who specialize in other media), and amateurs as well, because it presents a personal, spontaneous way of working with materials that are easy to obtain. A wealth of books on the discipline of collage is available to those who wish to study its origins and development. This book provides information on paper and fabric collage, collagraphy, and found object collage, to assist and inspire both those who are just discovering the medium of collage, and those who would like to add to their knowledge and skills. As you will see, the creative possibilities of working with collage are infinite.

A SHORT HISTORY
of Collage

C. P. Kunstadt
In Reverence
Collage with mixed media
4" x 6" (10 cm x 15 cm)

Ellen Wineberg
White Bird on Black
Collage with oil and shards on wood
12" x 15" (30 cm x 38 cm)

In 1912, Pablo Picasso and Georges Braque began making paper collages according to the principles of cubism. Their two-dimensional collages employed newspaper clippings, colored papers, tobacco wrappers, and wallpapers. They favored printed papers with trompe l'oeil patterns resembling materials such as wood grains and chair caning, and they often embellished their works with painted details or charcoal drawings.

Once the cubists adopted collage, other artists and movements recognized its potential. In Italy, the futurists used collage to convey the ideals of the machine age—speed, dynamism, and mechanization. Russian constructivists employed collage in the posters that heralded the Russian Revolution. Dadaists and surrealists of the 1920s stretched the boundaries of the medium, incorporating found objects, mixing elevated subject matter with mundane or earthy topics, and placing texts or headlines in unusual contexts to impart new meaning to them.

Marcel Duchamp, the most well known Dadaist, created "ready-mades," found objects to which he added text. His most scandalous ready-made, entitled Fountain, was fashioned from a urinal and bore this signature: R. Mutt. Duchamp also created collages that combined his own artwork with mass-produced images. Two other well known Dada artists, Kurt Schwitters and Max Ernst, used collage extensively. Schwitters integrated memorabilia from his personal life (tickets, newspapers, letters) into his collages. Ernst, deeply interested in the new field of psychiatry, employed the principle of automatism—suspending the conscious mind's control in order to release subconscious images. Collage enabled him to access these images and render them in his work. Ernst achieved subtle effects by exploiting the medium of paper, using tracings and rubbings, as well as damaging certain images in his work through peeling or tearing.

The works of Joseph Cornell form a watershed in the history of collage. He created arrangements of objects— old bottles, toys, trinkets—in small boxes (these three-dimensional collages are often called assemblages), as well as working with paper images. Surrealistic juxtapositions, such as the printed image of a human being's body topped with the head of a bird, are a hallmark of his work. Though associated with the surrealists, he also cited the influence of Hans Christian Andersen's *Great Screen* (1662), which combined paper cutouts of outdoor scenes, architectural elements, and myriad faces on a large folding screen.

In the 1940s, abstract expressionists appropriated collage to express the pioneering spirit of the artist. Robert Motherwell adapted paper collage to generate abstract forms from materials such as wine bottle labels, soap boxes, book jackets, and cigarette packages, typically emphasizing torn edges. He considered collage to be a form of play, a medium that allowed him to be gestural and spontaneous. Robert Rauschenberg, however, used collage techniques to challenge the abstract expressionists' devotion to pristine surfaces and nonrepresentational themes in his "combine paintings" such as *Bed* (1955), which featured a mattress and bedclothes that have been painted.

Jasper Johns continued the development of collage in the 1950s with three-dimensional pieces often incorporating dartboards (their concentric circles recur as a motif in his work) and other large items, such as molds of heads. He frequently embellished these works with paint. During the pop art movement of the 1960s, collage artists focused on items representing pop culture, such as televisions sets, advertisements, telephones, comic strips, and food packaging— variously spoofing them, transforming them, or giving them an eerie life of their own. For example, Claes Oldenberg's large-scale soft sculptures re-create everyday objects in unusual materials, such as a huge ice cream cone rendered in fuzzy fabric.

More recently, neo-Expressionists have incorporated collage elements into primarily painted surfaces. Julian Schnabel, for example, has attached crockery to his painted canvases. Jeff Koons has continued to interpret elements of pop culture, as in his treatment of a balloon twisted into an animal shape and cast in ceramic with a metallic finish. Collage also well expresses the postmodern nonlinear view of time, in which fragments of the past can overlap with the present. The viewer can consider the meaning of an item in its original context as well as the ramifications of its new position.

Clara Wainwright
Out of Order
Paper with mixed media
54" x 54" (137 cm x 137 cm)

Betty Guernsey
Every Time We Say Goodbye
Paper with mixed media
20" x 30" (51 cm x 76 cm)

COLLAGE BASICS

BASIC TECHNIQUES

When working with paper, it is important to choose your adhesives carefully. Rubber cement should be avoided because over time it dries out and loses its ability to hold. Acid-free glues such as PVA will dry clear and won't stain papers as they age. Many collage artists use acrylic mediums (available in matte or gloss finish) to adhere papers because they dry clear, are easy to use, and can add translucency to light papers such as tissue or rice paper. When working with any kind of paper or board support, always coat both sides first with acrylic medium to keep the support from warping.

Many artists use acid-free papers where possible, but most found papers (newspapers, magazines, vintage papers) aren't pH-neutral. You can minimize discoloration by encasing pieces in acrylic medium, but it's likely they will still change over time. This is no reason to avoid them—found papers add character to your work and their ephemeral nature is part of their charm.

For assemblages, use industrial-strength craft glues such as E6000 for adhering heavy objects, metal, and other nonporous surfaces. And be open to alternative ways of joining materials: Transparent or masking tape, straight pins, staples, string, thread, wire, tacks, grommets, and brads are all effective and also add interesting details and textures to a piece.

BASIC COLLAGE SUPPLIES

In addition to the materials specified for each project, you'll need to have the following basic collage supplies on hand: newspapers to protect your work area, scissors (small and large), a craft knife and self-healing cutting mat, brayer, metal ruler, pencil and eraser, artist's and foam paintbrushes in assorted sizes, water jar, paint palette, and a hair dryer (for cutting drying time). Susan Pickering Rothamel, author of *The Art of Paper Collage*, recommends using a viewfinder—an empty picture-framing mat—to aid in the composition of your piece.

Most of the projects require access to photocopiers and several entail computers and black-and-white or color printers. We assume people will have the following common household items on hand: paper towels, rags, tweezers, cotton balls and swabs, rubbing alcohol, masking tape, and a stapler, as well as basic tools such as a hammer, screwdrivers, wire cutters, needle-nose pliers, and sandpaper.

GLOSSARY OF BASIC TERMS

APPLIQUÉ—To form a design or motif by sewing shaped pieces of fabric on a foundation fabric.

ASSEMBLAGE—Sculptural or three-dimensional collage that is made by assembling diverse materials and found objects.

CHINE COLLÉ—A process whereby thin papers are collaged onto printmaking paper during the printing process. The papers are placed on the inked plate, glue side up, with the printing paper on top. The plate and papers are then run through the press thereby both gluing and printing the papers.

COLLAGE—Artwork that is created by adhering images, materials, and ephemera onto a surface.

ENCAUSTIC—An ancient technique of painting with pigmented hot wax.

FROTTAGE—Taking a rubbing of a textured surface to generate a design.

GESSO—A mixture of plaster and glue or size that is used as a background for paintings (or in sculpture).

GOUACHE—An opaque, matte water-based paint.

LAUAN—¼" (½ cm) plywood veneer, often used as a support for encaustic.

MONOPRINT—A print made from a painted printing plate with elements such as texture or imagery repeated in successive prints. Each print is unique because it is painted in varying ways each time it is printed.

MONOTYPE—A print made from a painted Plexiglas plate to produce a one-of-a-kind image.

MONTAGE—The technique of assembling, overlaying, and overlapping many different materials to create an image or artwork.

PHOTOMONTAGE—The technique of combining several photographs or parts of photographs to create a composite picture or artwork.

PHOTO TRANSFER—A process by which an image is transferred from a photocopy to another surface using solvent, acrylic medium, or transfer paper.

PVA GLUE—Polyvinyl acetate; an archival adhesive that is transparent when dry and is excellent for working with papers of varied weights and textures.

VELLUM—Refers to the translucent vellum papers available in many colors and patterns in art supply stores.

Paper
COLLAGE

Although there are many varieties of paper collage, they all begin with the same simple materials: pieces of paper and glue. These two everyday items offer nearly endless possibilities for combining colors, patterns, and textures. Paper collage is popular because its techniques are easy to learn and its materials are inexpensive and readily available. In addition to fresh sheets of colored or painted paper of various weights and textures, a host of common items may be recycled into collage, including magazines, newspapers, grocery bags, letters, tickets, gift wrap, confetti, receipts, paper towels, labels, train schedules, wax paper, posters, and so on. Artists who work in other media often layer old sketches, drafts, and leftover pieces of artwork into collage. The result may be a sophisticated work of fine art or a simple greeting card.

◀ **Helen Orth**
Collage Mystique
Paper collage
35" x 25" (64 cm x 64 cm)

▲ **Gordon Carlisle**
Leap
Collage with acrylic painting enhancement
5.5" x 3.5" (14 cm x 8 cm)

Collage artists may also manipulate paper to achieve a variety of effects. Folding, tearing, crumpling, cutting (perhaps with pinking shears), wetting, puncturing, and embellishing with lead pencil or paints can lend expressiveness and visual interest. Also, the arrangement of collage elements is as important as the selection of papers. Many people enjoy the spontaneous process of mixing the papers randomly until a pleasing composition is achieved. Still, a consideration of design basics—line, color, shape, pattern, size, value, and movement—will enhance the final product. In collage, the design process is simplified because the materials can be rearranged several times before they are glued down.

Paper collage had a long history as a folk art before emerging as a fine art in the twentieth century. For example, it was used to decorate twelfth-century Japanese calligraphic texts and nineteenth-century German greeting cards. Families of the Victorian period collected the ephemera of everyday life, including calling cards, newspaper headlines, invitations, and greeting cards, and then arranged it in parlor scrapbooks—thus creating collage. During the twentieth century, paper collages gained prominence in the cubist, dadaist, and surrealist movements. At the same time, it continued its role as an approachable medium that excludes no one, celebrating the multiplicity of images, texts, and papers (commonplace, bizarre, humorous, and beautiful ones) that surround us.

This chapter features the work of contemporary artists Rachel Paxton and Karen L. McCarthy. Paxton approaches her collages without a precise subject in mind. She uses collage as a method of working, a process through which she arrives at an expression of an idea, feeling, or impression to share with viewers. McCarthy approaches collage from the opposite position. She begins with a definite topic or idea in mind and builds upon it. Both artists incorporate techniques from other media: Paxton uses painting, and McCarthy employs her background in sewing.

▲ **Timothy Harney**
Green Chair and Stolen Flowers
Paper with acrylic and mixed media
14" x 11" (55 cm x 46 cm)
Courtesy of the artist and Clark Gallery

Paper MATERIALS

Although a primitive paper made of bark was

used by the people of Mexico and Central America in pre-Columbian times, paper that we would recognize as such today was developed in China, where papermaking evolved into a high art. Paper is composed of fibers that have been compressed into a compact web. Handmade paper has four deckle edges (uncut edges with a soft contour). Mold-made paper, created on a very long screen and then cut by machine, has two deckle edges. Machine-made paper, produced on huge screens and then cut, has no deckle edges.

Handmade papers are considered the finest. Mold-made and machine-made papers, even when produced from the same fibers, are generally inferior to handmade papers. Most handmade paper in the West is made from cotton linters (waste fiber remaining after ginning) and cotton rags (longer, tougher waste fiber remaining after the thread-making process—hence the name rag paper). These papers offer a wide variety of texture, color, and finish. A typical sheet might be 22 by 30 inches or 32 by 44 inches in dimension, though much smaller sizes can also be found. Unique handmade paper might feature wildflowers, shredded currency, or glitter, which can lend a unique effect to a collage.

Japan's handmade papers are the most highly prized. There are three main types: *Casey, gampi* and *mitsumata*.

▲ Eloise Pickard Smith
Little Old Ladies Home
Paper and fabric with found objects
18.75" x 18.25" (48 cm x 46 cm)

Casey is the strongest and has the longest fibers, which can clearly be seen in the paper. Gampi fibers, also long, are thinner and glossier, creating a tough, translucent paper. Mitsumata is composed of short fibers harvested from the bark of a shrub; it offers a soft, semigloss surface. Both gampi and mitsumata papers are naturally insect resistant.

Other Asian countries produce high-quality handmade paper. In the Philippines, the leaf fiber abaca and grass fibers such as bamboo, rice, and rattan are sources for papermaking. A long tradition of Himalayan papermaking exists, employing bast fibers taken from the inner bark of a tree commonly referred to as the "paper tree."

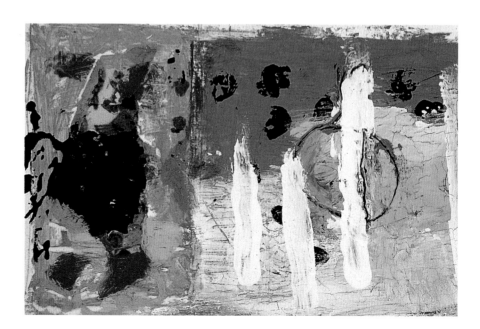

▶ Susan Gartrell
Blackbird
Paper with mixed media
4.5" x 9.25" (11 cm x 24 cm)

Photo by Kay Canavino

Its fibers can be harvested without killing the plant, an important benefit in the environmentally endangered Himalayan forests. In India, handmade paper is produced from a variety of fibers—khadi (a long-fiber cotton), recycled jute sacking (gunny paper), sugarcane fiber, banana leaf fiber, rice husks, and tea, algae, and wool fibers.

Certain features of a paper should be weighed when considering it for a particular use in collage. A paper's texture (determined by its fibers), its thickness (resulting from how heavily the pulp was applied to the screen), and its shape and size (determined by the size of the screen or how the paper was cut) will influence an artist's choices. Thick, opaque, machine-made papers might form a collage's base; translucent, delicate papers can be layered on the surface. Medium-weight papers can serve many purposes because they are thin enough to fold easily, yet thick enough to hold their position and shape.

In collage, the artist can celebrate paper's richness as an expressive medium, whether working with comic strips, wallpaper, dress patterns, catalogs, sheet music, stamps, poster board, maps, ruled notebook paper, playing cards, playbills, or handmade art papers. Exploring a variety of papers and their special characteristics and possibilities is one of the pleasures of collage work.

▲ **Rachel Paxton**
Between Noon and Sunset #22
Paper with mixed media
19" x 15" (48 cm x 38 cm)

◀ **Eloise Pickard Smith**
Vessel
17.5" x 24.5" (45 cm x 62 cm)

Paper
TECHNIQUES

To begin a paper collage you will need some basic

supplies; for cutting, you will need scissors, a safety ruler, knife blades in a variety of sizes, and a cutting mat. Cutting mats are usually made of firm rubber that grips the paper, ensuring control as you cut and providing a clean edge. You also must choose the best glue for your project. Rubber cement may minimize rippling and puckering, but be careful—its bond is not permanent, and papers applied with it can be peeled off. Other possibilities include PVA glues such as Elmer's Glue-All and Sobo Premium Craft & Fabric Glue; you might also use a glue stick. Acrylic gel affixes papers well and is transparent when it dries. Each glue suits different tasks and thicknesses of paper; in fact, a combination of different glues might be used in a single project. Before assembling your collage, experiment with scrap papers to determine which glue works best with your materials. (Refer to Collage Basics, page 12, for additional information.)

Next, take out the collage materials you have gathered: family pictures, postcards, craft paper, envelopes with postmarked stamps, old magazines from the attic, gift bags, construction paper, specialty papers, old birthday cards, crossword puzzles, and so on. Find a large, clean surface on which to work, and cover it with newsprint or brown paper to protect it from glue. Place the "background" sheet of paper on this surface. It is usually best for the novice to begin with a small sheet.

Next, choose one piece to form the focus of the work. Consider its text or image, its texture, and its color. Before you do any gluing, choose the rest of the pieces and rearrange the papers until you are satisfied with the result. Some collage artists prefer to cut collage pieces in a pattern. Use newsprint or brown paper to create a template, and then lightly trace the pattern onto the collage papers.

To avoid pencil lines on the front of the collage, trace the pattern on the back of each paper, but be sure to place the pattern piece facedown as well, to ensure the correct result. Then carefully cut out the collage pieces.

You can manipulate the paper pieces in various ways before affixing them to the collage surface. Cutting paper produces a clean edge; use a narrow, pointed knife blade on delicate papers and a razor blade or X-Acto knife on thicker papers, such as poster board. Folding paper creates a softer straight edge, with some relief. Tearing paper, unless you use a ruler, will not result in a straight edge but produces a random, spontaneous feeling. Paper can also be crumpled, punctured, wetted, or decorated with paints, color pencils, block prints, and so on.

Get ready to glue the pieces into place after you are pleased with the overall composition of the collage and the shape, texture, and decoration of each piece. Keep a damp cloth or paper towel ready, to wipe excess glue off your hands as you work. Plan

before you begin; it might be best to affix the larger background pieces first, and then add the details. Or you may wish to assemble complicated elements of the design, such as a flower with petals made of different papers, before securing them to the collage.

Coat one of your collage pieces evenly and sparingly with glue. A brush will be useful if you are using a runny glue. Then apply it smoothly to the collage, using gentle pressure with the heel of your hand. You might place a cloth or paper between your hand and the collage, to keep the surface clean. Carefully follow this process with each piece, and the collage will take shape neatly before your eyes. Let the piece dry completely before adding the finishing touches—a bit of painted or penciled color, another paper detail or two, a light acrylic wash, or whatever your work of art inspires you to do.

▲ **Susan Gartrell**
Easter Island
Paper with mixed media
5" x 6.5" (13 cm x 17 cm)

◀ **Timothy Harney**
The Piano Room
Paper with acrylic and mixed media
13.75" x 16.75" (35 cm x 43 cm)
Courtesy of the artist and Clark Gallery

▶ **Robin Chandler**
Genesis, Genesis
Paper collage
38" x 48" (86 cm x 122 cm)
Photo by Kay Canavino

RACHEL PAXTON

TROMPE L'OEIL
Paper Collage

Pattern and the relationship between art, nature,

and spirituality have been the focus of Rachel Paxton's work for the past 15 years. Her paper collages address life, death, and the passage of time, and they project a calm, contemplative atmosphere. They also reflect her allegiance to a time when humanity held greater respect for nature, craft, and religion.

Although Paxton once constructed painted abstract assemblages (three-dimensional collages) made from found objects and wood, she now concentrates on collages that are composed of paper only. Still, her background as a trained textile designer is evident in her work. She creates small paintings that simulate specific types of fabrics—striped mattress ticking and nineteenth-century wallpaper designs inspired by William Morris, for example—and affixes them to her collages. Her ability as a painter shows in the carefully rendered details. By using block prints of certain designs rather than hand-rendering them, she creates a consistent pattern. She prints her designs on beige or gray Arches paper or on tissue paper, to

which she later adds texture by crumpling or painting.

In her most recent work, Paxton has examined the passage of time by using fruit still life as a metaphor for the cycle of human life. She uses a number of techniques to evoke the passage of time. Coffee-dyeing gives an aged quality to certain papers; she simply soaks the paper in coffee for a few minutes and then lets it dry naturally. The result is much like "foxing," the browning effect produced by the aging process in papers that contain wood acid. Since foxing typically affects older paper, this type of staining is recognized as antique. Elements such as old sheet music and faux vintage fabric lend an air of antiquity to her collages. For the viewer, these familiar objects from the past evoke memories and create a feeling of nostalgia.

Paxton also tries to produce a sense of altered space in her collages. Although the background of her work is flat, Paxton introduces shadowing in the fruit still life to disorient the viewer, who seems to be positioned both within and above the collage. This juxtaposition expresses the discomfiting relationship between the past and the present, as well as the shifting nature of human perception.

◀ *Pinwheel Chamber, Late Afternoon*
Paper with mixed media
32" x 40" (81 cm x 102 cm)

MATERIALS

- acrylic paints in a variety of colors

- assorted specialty papers

- containers for mixing

- easel

- matte acrylic gel

- newsprint

- number 2 pencils

- paintbrushes

- palette knife

- paper palette

- paper towels

- printmaking paper (such as Arches) in buff

- scissors or other cutting tools

- spotlight

In preparing to create a paper collage, the artist chooses from her stores of gravestone rubbings, old sheet music, tracings of wallpaper, block prints with motifs adapted from fabric designs, and coffee-dyed nautical maps.

Tinting Paper

In addition to tinting paper with coffee, you can try other liquids to produce a variety of hues. Green tea produces a nice effect.

1 For the preliminary design, Paxton lays out the paper painted with a mattress ticking pattern, sheet music, and crumpled tissue printed with repeating pattern motifs. She tears and cuts the original sheets to create textural interest and a balanced composition. She then fine-tunes the composition by cutting or tearing small bits of paper and by rearranging and adding pieces.

2 Paxton glues the bottom layer into place first; she turns the torn paper over onto a pile of clean newsprint, which keeps the edges of the collage free of excess glue. She then applies acrylic gel with a 1 1/2-inch brush, using strokes that radiate from the center of the paper to the edges, covering the paper completely. Paxton then places the piece onto the collage and makes it adhere smoothly by applying even pressure with the heel of her hand. Placing a piece of clean tissue paper over the freshly glued paper before pressure is applied will keep the surface clean. After all the papers have been glued into place, the collage is allowed to dry completely.

3 Next, Paxton applies acrylic gel to portions of the crumpled rice paper, which was glued over the block print pattern for textural interest. After it dries, the acrylic gel resists the light acrylic wash that she is shown brushing over the surface, thus leaving some areas untinted. This subtle coloring heightens the textured effect of the crumpled paper.

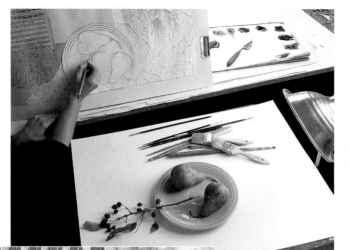

4 At this point, a difficult stage of the process begins—the addition of the painted still life. Paxton determines the position of the fruit on the plate and the placement of shadows by looking at the still life from above, under direct light. Once the composition of the still life and its placement have been decided, the artist sketches it directly onto the collage, using a number 2 pencil.

5 The artist now begins to paint the still life onto the collage with acrylic paint, which is easily mixed and water soluble. She begins this process only after the acrylic gel and subsequent washes have dried completely.

Making a Deckle Edge
To create the look of a deckle edge, use a ruler when tearing the paper pieces. This ensures a straight edge but produces a soft effect.

Texture Tip

If you plan to crumple a piece of paper, cut it slightly larger (by $1/8$ inch to $1/4$ inch) than the area it is intended to cover, to allow for shrinkage after crumpling.

6 Once the still life is completed, Paxton goes back into the collage to balance the overall effect by adding paper or adjusting painted areas with small amounts of color.

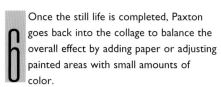

7 In the final step of the process, the artist adds depth and an aged effect by enhancing the torn and deckle edges of the paper with a light brown acrylic wash. The completed collage is a product of tearing, gluing, painting, and balancing.

KAREN L. McCARTHY

WOVEN
Paper Collage

Karen L. McCarthy's paper collages express

her exploration of the tension between clarity, order, and specificity, on one hand, and the ambiguity of abstract forms. She seeks to convey spatial depth through rich surface texture. She finds that paper as a medium lends spontaneity to her work, enabling her to rework surfaces, to build up media, and to add depth.

American quilts, Japanese landscape design, and the undulating pathways that pattern many board games have influenced McCarthy's work. Most recently, she has focused on American artists and writers of the nineteenth and twentieth centuries; several of her collages pay homage to particular individuals whom she finds intriguing or inspiring. Her designs mix sinuous lines with repetitive, structured patterns. McCarthy's distinctive use of paste paper, a textured paper that she creates herself by applying homemade, dyed cornstarch paste to papers, imbues her collages with a multiplicity of pattern and color.

In the piece entitled *Pushing Up New Roots: For Edith Wharton*, McCarthy reflects upon Wharton's concerns about intellectual growth and repression in turn-of-the-century American society. The title refers to a letter that Wharton wrote to Bernard Berenson, in which she questioned the ability of human beings to "push up new roots." The work is alive with movement, suggesting that growth comes at the cost of pushing through barriers and grappling with conflict.

◄ *Pushing Up New Roots:*
For Edith Wharton
Paper with pigmented cornstarch, thread, and colored pencil
26" x 26" (66 cm x 66 cm)

MATERIALS

acrylic and metallic paints

colored pencils

compass

cornstarch paste (see recipe on page 35)

fabric paint

graphite tracing paper

number 2 pencils

paintbrush (1-inch flat)

papers for making paste paper

printmaking paper for backing

ruler

scissors or other cutting tools

Scotch Magic Tape

sewing machine (domestic or industrial model)

thread

white PVA glue (such as Sobo Premium Craft & Fabric Glue)

Paste and Paper

Many papers work well as a base for paste paper; even handmade papers will do the job, but they must be handled carefully or they will rip. Printmaking papers sometimes absorb too much moisture from the paste, yet they are very nice for reworking with lead or colored pencils. Try a variety of papers to find which you prefer. A list of suggestions follows:

Arches

Canson Mi-Teintes (in colors and in white)

Rives

Strathmore Bristol (in 1-ply kid finish)

Strathmore Charcoal (in colors and in white)

blender

cooking pot

cornstarch (1 cup)

disposable plastic cups

**liquid pigments
(such as Guerra)**

plastic spoons

rubber gloves

stove or hot plate

strainer

water

McCarthy uses a traditional method of making pigmented cornstarch paste. She adds cornstarch to a pot of boiling water, stirs constantly until it thickens, and then lets it cool to a gel. Then she colors the paste with liquid pigments.

KAREN L. McCARTHY'S CORNSTARCH PASTE RECIPE

Dissolve 1 cup of cornstarch into 1 cup of room-temperature water. Place the mixture in a pot, and heat it slowly. Gradually add 3 more cups of water to the mixture, and continue heating, stirring constantly, until the mixture boils. (Caution: bubbles may pop messily; be careful!) While stirring, boil the mixture for 2 to 3 minutes, until it is thick and forms a gel. Let it cool completely.

Remove 1 cup of the mixture, and place it in a blender. Add 1 cup of water, and blend it until smooth; this makes a thin paste. Add less water if you would like a thicker paste for a particular project. Strain the paste before using it.

To add color, simply use a plastic spoon to stir paints or pigments into cups of paste. Never place pigmented paste into a blender that will be used for food preparation. Pigments stain easily and should be handled with care (wear rubber gloves). The paste will keep for several days if stored in the refrigerator or another cool place.

35

1 McCarthy brushes the cornstarch mixture onto the paper with a paintbrush, taking care to cover the surface completely. She makes patterns and textures on the surface with implements such as combs and cookie cutters, to add shadows, depth, and rhythm. She then allows the paper to dry completely. A second layer of color can be applied after the first one dries. Colors will lighten somewhat as they dry. The artist often spends a week at a time on this process, making enough pigment-dyed papers to last for a couple of months.

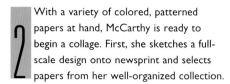

2 With a variety of colored, patterned papers at hand, McCarthy is ready to begin a collage. First, she sketches a full-scale design onto newsprint and selects papers from her well-organized collection.

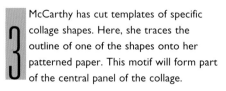

3 McCarthy has cut templates of specific collage shapes. Here, she traces the outline of one of the shapes onto her patterned paper. This motif will form part of the central panel of the collage.

4 After cutting out all the shapes, McCarthy adds shading and texture to their surfaces by reworking them with a variety of materials: fabric paint, paste, colored pencils, and acrylic and metallic paints.

5 At this stage, McCarthy glues the smallest collage pieces onto the larger squares. Although she has precisely drawn the collage's overall design, she often assembles the entire collage (using a bit of removable cellophane tape folded over and applied to the back of each piece) before beginning to glue the pieces together. Thus she can fine-tune her design as a visual whole and ensure the proper positioning of each piece.

6 Next, the artist considers where she will apply stitching to the collage. Then she assembles one section at a time, gluing the pieces on a paper backing cut to fit. After the glue has dried, she draws lines that will guide her stitching, using a pencil with a ruler or compass.

7 McCarthy stitches along the penciled lines. Working with small sections of the collage simplifies the machine sewing. She has already tested samples of the papers to determine proper needle size and tension—a step she considers absolutely essential. Needles that are too small may break; McCarthy often uses Schmetz jeans/denim number 16 needles for work with thick papers.

8 Once all the sections of the central panel are complete, McCarthy attaches them to the full-scale paper backing of the collage. She applies white PVA glue with a 1-inch brush, to make an even, spare application.

Stitch Tip

You might use hand stitching rather than machine stitching to embellish paper, for both practical and aesthetic reasons. Machine stitching can be awkward for larger works; hand stitching allows more freedom of choice in threads and yarn, and may yield a freer line. Hand stitching is, however, more time consuming.

9 Here the artist finishes the edges of the four central-panel squares with a zigzag stitch.

10 McCarthy next attaches the stitch-embellished border of the collage, using a minimal amount of glue. Individual pieces are weighted for drying, and to prevent wrinkling.

11 After the glued border has dried, McCarthy finishes the edge between the central panel and the border with a zigzag topstitch. Because the entire collage must be handled to complete this final step, great care must be taken not to bend or wrinkle the delicate papers. McCarthy's background in sewing serves her well here.

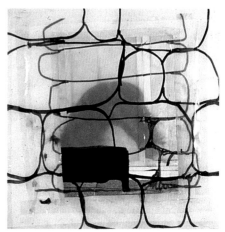

◀ **Gina Occhiogrosso**
After Millay
Mixed media paper collage
18" x 20" (46 cm x 51 cm)

▼ **Gina Occhiogrosso**
Untitled
Mixed media vellum collage
14" x 14" (36 cm x 36 cm)

Eloise Pickard Smith ▶
Hanaogi
22.5" x 30" (57 cm x 76.2 cm)

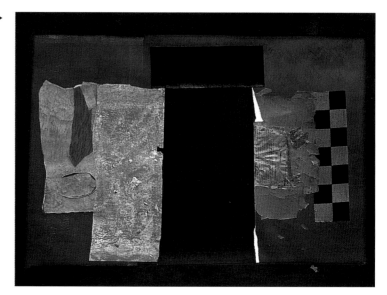

GALLERY

◀ **Felicia Belair-Rigdon**
Untitled
Mixed media collage with handmade paper
30" x 39" (76 cm x 99 cm)

Felicia Belair-Rigdon ▲
From a Long Time Ago
Mixed media collage with handmade paper
24" x 32" (61 cm x 81 cm)

◀ **Susan Gartrell**
Woods Hill
Paper with mixed media
4" x 4" (10 cm x 10 cm)

Photo by Kay Canavino

▲ **Gordon Carlisle**
Lady of the Lake
Collage with acrylic painting enhancement
12" x 8.75" (30 cm x 22 cm)

▼ **Gordon Carlisle**
Repose
Collage with acrylic painting enhancement
3.5" x 5.5" (9 cm x 14 cm)

▲ **Karen McCarthy**
Moksha-Patamu: For Beatrice Wood
Paper with pigmented starch paste, thread, and colored pencil
26" x 26" (66 cm x 66 cm)

Rachel Paxton ▶
Pinwheels & Pears, Early Morning
Paper with mixed media
21" x 38" (53 cm x 97 cm)

▼ **Nancy Virbila**
Summer Sun
Paper with mixed media
20" x 16" (51 cm x 40 cm)

▲ **Nancy Virbila**
Porter's Woods
Paper with mixed media
20" x 24" (51 cm x 61 cm)

▼ **Robin Chandler**
The Lesser Peace #9
Paper collage
18" x 24" (46 cm x 61 cm)

▲ **Robin Chandler**
The Lesser Peace #6
Paper collage
18" x 24" (46 cm x 61 cm)

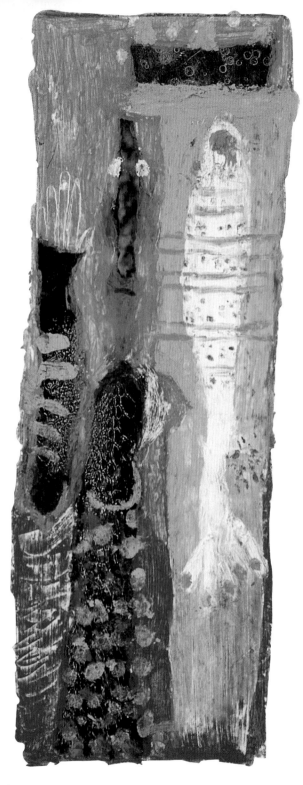

▲ **Susan Gartrell**
Catch of the Day
Paper with mixed media
3.5" x 9.25" (9 cm x 23 cm)

Photo by Kay Canavino

▶ **Timothy Harney**
Orange + Lemon
Paper with acrylic and mixed media
5.5" x 9.25" (14 cm x 23 cm)
Courtesy of artist and Clark Gallery

▼ **Timothy Harney**
Late August and an Orange Bowl
Paper with acrylic and mixed media
11.25" x 7" (29 cm x 18 cm)
Courtesy of artist and Clark Gallery

▲ **Timothy Harney**
Circus (Still Life for John Grillo)
Paper with acrylic and mixed media
22" x 18.25" (56 cm x 46 cm)
Courtesy of artist and Clark Gallery

Fabric
COLLAGE

In fabric collage, one piece of fabric is affixed to another either by gluing or by sewing. As in other forms of collage, the color, textures, and patterns of the materials make the end result interesting. Because glue does not secure fabric as permanently as sewing does, many artists choose to sew their collages together, which requires excellent sewing skills and makes the process more challenging. Materials for this medium are readily available: scraps from other sewing projects, remnants (especially decorator fabrics), vintage clothing, old tablecloths and linens (from antique stores, flea markets, or a grandparent's linen closet), upholstery fabric, and, of course, new fabric purchased off the bolt.

As a domestic art, sewing is intimately linked to women, and it is no coincidence that most fabric collage artists today are women.

Linda Perry
Approaching Storm
Fabric with found objects
40" x 57" (102 cm x 145 cm)
Photo by Joe Ofría

▲ **Dominie Nash**
Peculiar Poetry 9
44" x 44.5" (112 cm x 113 cm)

Fabric collage developed from the tradition of quilting, enriched by its emphasis on unifying diverse patterns and shapes, achieving excellence in stitchery, and gathering up seemingly insignificant fragments and scraps to rework them into a new functional and beautiful creation. The two disciplines are closely related and in fact overlap—much of the work of contemporary quilters incorporates elements of fabric collage, just as fabric collage artists have borrowed from the tradition of quilting. Some fabric collage artists began their creative work with fabric in the area of traditional quilting, whereas artists from other backgrounds have simply acquired solid sewing skills before delving into the medium of fabric collage.

Although fabric has been incorporated into other collage

disciplines (for example, Picasso and Braque employed it in their cubist collages), collage created primarily of fabric has developed more recently. It lends itself both to the production of functional pieces, such as pillow covers, handbags, apparel, and quilts, as well as to the creation of fine art.

Both of this chapter's featured artists, Clara Wainwright and Sandra Donabed, have a traditional sewing background; Donabed is also an experienced quilter. Both artists have moved away from traditional methods of working with cloth, taking a fresh look at their materials and stretching the boundaries of convention. Whimsical juxtapositions and an improvisational spirit make these works vibrant, thought provoking, and fun.

Therese May
Queen of Clubs
Embellished quilt
18" x 28" (46 cm x 71 cm)

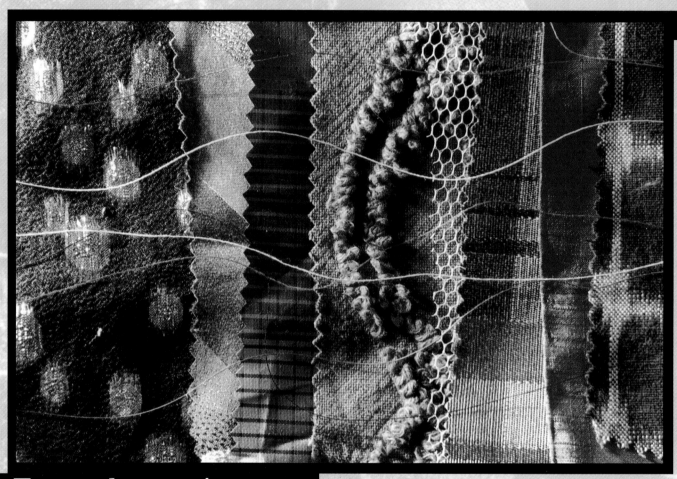

Fabric AND FIBER

Probably the best fabric choice for the beginning

collage artist is firmly woven cotton, such as broadcloth or muslin; you might choose solids, stripes, calico, gingham, or other patterns. But, though the rainbow of cotton yardage in a quilting shop may supply all an artist needs to begin, exploring other fibers and weaves really opens up the possibilities of working in this medium. Sheer organza (perhaps with iridescent fibers woven in), chenilles (woven from a plush yarn), drapey velvets, damask (a dense fabric with woven-in patterns), open-weave cottons that might be layered over another fabric, moirés (with a rippled watermark finish), netting, cottons woven with metallic threads, lace yardage, raw silk, terry cloth, different weights of linen, corduroy, shiny taffeta—the list of choices is endless. Studying the visual and tactile properties of various fabrics is an ongoing part of creating fabric collage.

In addition to the fabric store, popular sources of fabric for collage include the antique shop and flea market. Vintage materials from old dresses, doilies, embroidered handkerchiefs, neckties, banners, table linens, or laces can be sources of inspiration. You can also create an antique effect by using widely available fabric reproductions of old patterns, such as eighteenth-century block prints or art deco motifs. Think about recycling items from the attic as well, such as a swatch of your much-patched jeans from 1968 or a decal cut from an old T-shirt.

Decorator fabrics offer a trove of ideas for collage. Chintz, a cotton finished with sizing that imparts a sheen to it, is available in solids, prints (both tiny and baroque in scale), stripes, and plaids.

◄ **Jane Burch Cochran**
Life Line
Embellished quilt
82" x 68" (208 cm x 173 cm)
Photo by Pam Monfort

Though the sizing makes precise cutting simple, it will be lost if the chintz is laundered. Tapestry, a dense fabric often used in upholstery, is typically woven with intricate pictorial designs that might form the focus or background of a collage. Drapery fabrics, both heavy and sheer, present textures and patterns ranging from nubbly open-weave bouclés to heavy fabric printed with bright pop art designs.

Though most fabrics available today are machine-made, you might incorporate handmade or hand-decorated cloth to lend a unique touch to your work. The Asian traditions of *ikat* and *batik* are especially interesting. Ikat features mottled patterns that bleed into one another, an effect created by painting or tie-dyeing the threads of the warp or the weft—or both—before weaving. Batik fabric is patterned through wax-resist dyeing, typically yielding abstract, geometric, or floral designs. To add richness to your work, you might experiment with brilliantly dyed silks from India. Also, artisans in your local area might weave or dye specialty fabrics for you.

On the other end of the spectrum, fabrics that are considered strictly utilitarian can be appropriated for use in collage. Items as disparate as burlap feed bags, hair nets, a dishcloth, nylon stockings, quilt batting, cutouts from a sheet of vinyl, or a piece of a canvas sneaker might suit a particular topic or theme you'd like to explore—or inject a note of humor.

If you choose to sew your collage, the stitching can form a hidden part of the work's structure or may take a

more prominent role. For displayed stitching, your choice of thread or yarn becomes an important part of the design process. Standard cotton, polyester, and silk machine-sewing threads might suit a project, but other possibilities should also be considered: metallic threads, shiny mercerized cotton, matte cotton embroidery floss, or silk monofilament for hand stitching extremely delicate vintage fabrics. Be sure to determine whether a thread is suitable for handwork or machine stitching, and use it accordingly.

Finally, sewing notions such as braid, bias tape, ribbon, piping, and other trimmings are readily available in fabric shops to enhance your collages.

Though you might come to favor a particular type of fabric, explore them all!

▲ **Clara Wainwright**
Icbal's Vision
29.5" x 43" (75 cm x 109 cm)

Fabric
TECHNIQUES

To begin a fabric collage, you will need some

basic tools and materials. Find a few pairs of sharp scissors, including a small pair for delicate fabrics and detail work, and a large pair for cutting broad areas and thicker pieces of fabric. Pinking shears might be used to create an interesting cut edge. An iron is also necessary because, unfortunately, most fabrics have a tendency to wrinkle! Also, stock up on needles, threads in a variety of colors, sewing pins, a linen tape measure, a ruler, some tailor's chalk, a selection of soft pencils, and some tracing paper.

Next, gather your hoard of fabrics, and create a design. At a minimum, you will need a sketch to follow as you work. For your first project you might choose an image to reproduce in collage, such as a poster or a drawing of your own. Select fabrics that correspond to the image's

colors, shapes, or textures, such as yellow corduroy for wheat fields, green velour for fir trees, and shiny blue satin for the sky. Find a large piece of material for the background that might form part of the image or serve as a complementary border.

Next, cut out the individual shapes. You may use templates based on your design or work freehand. Treat fabric edges carefully; they can make the difference between a successful piece of work and a valiant but unsatisfactory effort. Edges of fabric can be finished in a number of ways: torn, cut, hemmed, bound, or topstitched. To tear a piece of fabric, make a small cut with sharp scissors, and then rip it gently. Cutting should be done carefully with scissors. Experiment with cutting or tearing a small swatch of your fabric to see whether the edge holds its shape or has a tendency to ravel; match your technique with the effect you want. Hemming makes a soft, finished edge with a bit of relief.

Binding—covering the edge with a separate piece of fabric—can be done in matching material or in a contrasting cloth. Like a hemmed edge, a bound edge offers a smooth finish with some relief. Topstitching secures edges neatly and helps to unify the elements of the collage.

You can embellish the individual pieces of your collage: Try fabric paint or embroidery; you may also stitch folds, tucks, or gathers into place. Extremely delicate items, such as a vintage fine lawn handkerchief, may need to be stitched carefully to a backing that will provide support.

The next step is to assemble all the pieces. Will you attach them to the background with glue or with sewing? If you choose sewing, decide whether to work by hand or by machine. You might use decorative embroidery stitches, such as chain stitch or feather stitch, to join the pieces. A machine zigzag stitch can connect the pieces while providing a neat edge that helps define each piece. Or you may prefer to keep the sewing invisible by seaming the pieces together with right sides facing each other (this works best with shapes bounded by lines, such as squares and rectangles; it is much trickier with curved shapes). Leave a $1/2$-inch

seam allowance when you cut the pieces, if you plan to use this technique (you can trim it after sewing).

If you intend to use glue, you might select Glue Stic, aerosol glue, Sobo Premium Craft & Fabric Glue, or heat-activated adhesives such as Stitch Witchery. Test the glues on scraps of your materials to determine which types work best and how much you should apply. A thick application of glue might cause discoloration of fine fabrics or puckering.

Also, decide on the order in which you'll attach the pieces to the background; you'll avoid some

headaches by thinking out a procedure in advance. You might stitch larger background pieces into place first and then apply the details by hand. Perhaps it would make more sense to complete small areas of the collage one at a time, joining these sections together as a final step.

After all the pieces have been secured, complete any finishing tasks, such as topstitching, quilting, backing the piece, or touching up details. All that remains is adding the border: perhaps a wide mitered "frame" of fabric, a narrow bound edge, or neatly turning the collage's edge to the back of the work and stitching it down to create a smooth, unadorned look.

▼ **Clara Wainwright**
Willendorf Inventory #1
Fabric collage
16" x 25" (41 cm x 64 cm)

◀ **Linda S. Perry**
Land, Sea and Sky
Fabric collage
60" x 48" (152 cm x 122 cm)
Photo by Joe Ofria

CLARA WAINWRIGHT

STORIES
in Stitches

Clara Wainwright uses fabric and sewing to

express her concerns about the fabric of society, especially the problems of famine, disease, and violence. She lifts these issues into the realm of art, where they can be considered philosophically and, she hopes, where insights might surface that could ultimately generate solutions. Despite the daunting issues she chooses to tackle, her work is instilled with a sense of hopefulness about life, particularly concerning women's ability to make the best of circumstances and to find beauty and joy in a confusing, conflicted world.

Wainwright's work is lyrical, combining fluidity of movement with arresting images. The exhilarating colors and liveliness of her collages reflect the influence of her favorite artists, Henri Matisse and Paul Gauguin. She also has been inspired by the humorous work of Paul Klee and the fantastic paintings of the sixteenth-century Dutch artist Hieronymus Bosch. She works intuitively, without detailed sketches or plans, and combines fabrics that vary in weight, texture, and color.

Wainwright began working in fabric collage with little formal training in art or design. But she knew how to sew, which gave her the confidence to plunge in. Her work encompasses diminutive pieces of an intimate scale, such as small pillows, and expansive creations, such as community quilts constructed in cooperation with adults and children. Her commitment to making a better world is evident both in the projects she takes on and in her fabric collages themselves, which acknowledge conflict and pain while projecting a buoyant hope.

◄ *Matisse Slept Here II*
Fabric collage
36" x 54" (91 cm x 137 cm)

MATERIALS

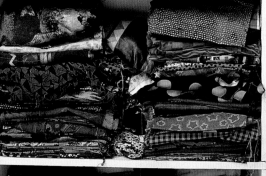

assorted fabrics

assorted threads to match or complement fabrics

fusible fabric adhesive (such as Stitch Witchery)

glue (such as Sobo Premium Craft & Fabric Glue, Elmer's Glue-All, or Glue Stic)

pins

quilted material for the backing of the collage

scissors

sewing machine (industrial or domestic model)

spray shoe polish

steam iron

Wainwright begins a fabric collage by browsing through her vast store of fabrics (she has been a collector for 20 years), much of it given to her by friends all over the world. Sometimes an image in a piece of material catches her eye and inspires an idea for a collage. Other designs and subject matter are inspired by the textures and patterns in various cloths.

1 Wainwright lays down the background fabric for the collage. Next, she cuts specific images and shapes from other pieces of material, arranging them on the background. She boldly combines stripes, checks, florals, solids, and abstract fabrics, balancing those that reflect light with others that absorb it. Here, she cuts an iridescent fabric with velvet stripes, which will serve as the hair of the figure in the collage.

2 Next, the artist applies black spray shoe polish to impart shading and dimension to a piece of fabric that will represent a vase.

Fabric and Art

As a subject for fabric collage, you might choose to reproduce a favorite work of art, simplifying its shapes, colors, and lines.

3 Wainwright dots white glue on a piece of fabric, using the smallest possible amount. She will let it dry a bit until it is tacky but not runny, before applying the piece; thus, the glue will secure the piece without seeping through the fabric to cause staining or rippling.

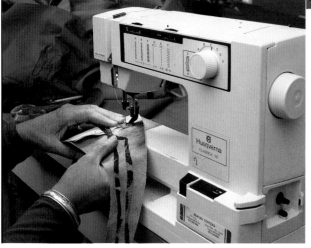

4 Wainwright now uses her sewing machine to stitch small details onto the larger pieces of the collage. All the details are sewn into place before the large pieces are joined.

Stitching Fragile Fabric

Certain fragile fabrics should be strengthened before being incorporated into a collage. You might use a fusible adhesive or a different fusible or stitch-applied backing to stabilize such pieces.

5 Wainwright applies a backing of fusible adhesive to a collage piece; when ironed, the adhesive will firmly adhere to the fabric. She will also use this adhesive to affix the large pieces of the collage to the background.

6 After all the components of the collage have been glued into place, the artist topstitches the pieces, completing the main panel of the work.

7 Wainwright adds stability to her fabric collages by attaching a ready-made quilted backing. She tacks it into place by hand with tiny, invisible stitches. To finish the piece, she attaches a decorative border.

SANDRA DONABED

VINTAGE
Work

Sandra Donabed made doll clothes as a child

and her own clothes as a young woman. She took an interest in quilting in the early 1980s, eventually focusing on the nontraditional methods of contemporary quilting. Her first effort in that style, a quilt inspired by a kindergarten photograph of her son, won first prize in a local show. Donabed's quilts often feature vintage fabric that she finds at yard sales and flea markets. She has cut up costumes and vintage clothing to use in her work and often purchases bolts of discontinued fabrics and designer chintz samples.

Autobiographical themes inform much of Donabed's work, and she addresses feminist issues through the use of domestic objects and subject matter. *The Writing on the Window* portrays a spiritual journey in search of fulfillment, grounded in familiar, homey materials and leavened with a touch of humor. Transforming simple domestic objects to represent a fundamental human aspiration shows Donabed's respect for the realm of home—traditionally a woman's domain—yet she employs them as a metaphor for seeking a vision for the future, not as a cozy, secure cocoon. The quilt's text was inspired by the lyrics of a Bob Marley song: "If it don't come gonna go looking for happiness."

Donabed likens her quilt-making process to the automatic writing of the surrealist painter Yves Tanguy. She believes that the artist does not control an artwork, but rather that the work emerges from the subconscious if the artist will release and nurture it. Donabed enjoys the process of discovery involved in making her quilts and feels that her understanding of a piece and its significance in her life are deepened by each step in its creation.

The Writing on the Window
Vintage cloth and other materials
62" x 62" (157 cm x 157 cm)
Photo by David Caras

MATERIALS

assortment of organza, cotton damasks, and chintzes

beads, rhinestones, and other adornments

cotton-covered polyester thread in assorted colors

cotton quilt batting (such as Fairfield)

lacy curtain panels

metallic thread

moiré fabric for backing

pins

scissors

sewing machines (both a domestic model and an industrial model for heavy work)

tea towels

vintage tablecloths

From her stash of vintage materials, Donabed chooses a large damask tablecloth to serve as the quilt's main design element—the grid of red bars resembles a window.

1 Donabed selects a number of complementary fabric samples and makes notes and sketches to explore ideas for her work. This part of the creative process will lead to a final drawing of the quilt.

2 The artist begins to construct the quilt by cutting the tablecloth fabric to form "windowpanes." She leaves enough of the white fabric to tuck under for a clean edge. A moiré fabric has been layered with an airy lace curtain panel to form the outdoor scene; sections of it are pinned into place within the windowpanes and then stitched.

3 Donabed often uses text in her quilts, which she creates by using a bias tape to form the letters. First she attaches the letters with pins and then sews them into place by hand. For this quilt she has chosen a fragile, bright blue organza for her lettering, cast in a graceful, longhand script.

4 Donabed has cut out large floral pieces from several fabrics to assemble this bouquet. She has attached these cutouts to one another with small areas of zigzag stitching; this secures the pieces so she can handle the bouquet as a single unit. She now pins the arrangement to a sheet of tissue paper to simplify moving it about on the background until she decides on its permanent position. After it is stitched into place, she will tear away the tissue paper.

5 Donabed uses a tight zigzag stitch to attach this cutout to the background fabric. Each element of the quilt is affixed in this fashion.

6 After finishing the assembly of all the quilt pieces, Donabed carefully pins together the layers of the quilt: the top, the batting that will serve as stuffing, and the moiré backing. In this painstaking process she ensures that the edges fit together perfectly and that the quilt is entirely smooth.

7 Donabed attaches 1-inch strips of the background material facedown on the edge of the front of the quilt. She then trims the batting and background material to the edge of the front of the quilt, and turns the 1-inch strip over, creating a hem on the reverse side of the piece. She stitches this down by hand, using a traditional hem stitch.

Making Bias Tape

You can make your own bias tape by choosing a lightweight fabric and cutting a length of it along the bias. Cut it about 1 inch wider than the desired width of the tape. Then tuck a $1/2$-inch allowance under on each side, and iron the tape. Use the tape for lettering or other effects.

Linda Perry ▶
Tuscany
Art quilts
40" x 58" (102 cm x 147 cm)
Photo by Joe Ofria

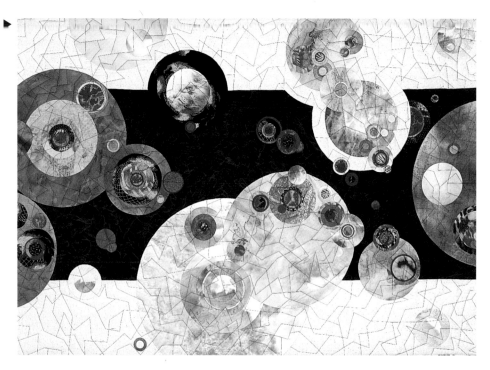

▼ **Linda Perry**
Faith and Time
Art quilts
42" x 48" (107 cm x 122 cm)
Photo by Joe Ofría

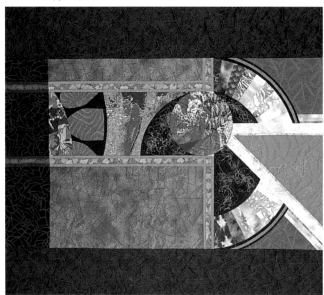

▲ **Dominie Nash**
Peculiar Poetry 8
43.5" x 42.5" (110 cm x 108 cm)

GALLERY

◄ **Therese May**
Hearts + Hands
Embellished quilt
20" x 20" (51 cm x 51 cm)

▼ **Therese May**
Child #6—Sandy
Embellished quilt
36" x 30" (91 cm x 76 cm)

▲ **Dominie Nash**
Sky Song 3
46" x 72" (117 cm x 183 cm)

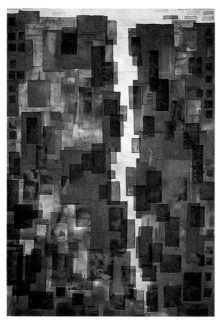

Erika Carter ▶
Confinement
Art quilt
65" x 45" (165 cm x 114 cm)

Erika Carter ▶
Reminiscent
Art quilt
60" x 44.5" (152 cm x 113 cm)

▲ **Barbara Mortenson**
Untitled
Fabric collage
3" x 5" (8 cm x 13 cm)

◀ **Barbara Mortenson**
Untitled
Fabric collage
3" x 5" (8 cm x 13 cm)

▼ ▶ Sandra Donabed
Hearts + Gizzards
Quilt with fabric collage
72" x 78" (183 cm x 198 cm)
(detail right)
Photos by David Caras

◀ Barbara Mortenson
Untitled
3" x 5" (8 cm x 13 cm)

▲ **Carol Andrews**
Untitled
Fabric with oil and wax on canvas
27" x 38" (69 cm x 97 cm)

▲ **Jane Burch Cochran**
Devotion
Embellished art quilt
68" x 85" (713 cm x 216 cm)

Photos by Pam Monfort

Jane Burch Cochran ▶
Life Starts Out So Simple
Embellished art quilt
68" x 68" (173 cm x 173 cm)

Photos by Pam Monfort

▲ **Carol Andrews**
Untitled
Fabric with watercolor, crayon, ink, latex,
and wrapping paper on canvas
23" x 30" (58 cm x 76 cm)

▲ **Clara Wainwright**
Waiting for Bosch
Fabric collage
26" x 22.5" (66 cm x 57 cm)

◀ **Clara Wainwright**
20th Anniversary Quilt for First Night
Fabric collage
100" x 77" (254 cm x 196 cm)

▲ **Clara Wainwright**
*Summer and Gauguin's Unanswered
Questions*
Fabric collage
48" x 108" (122 cm x 274 cm)

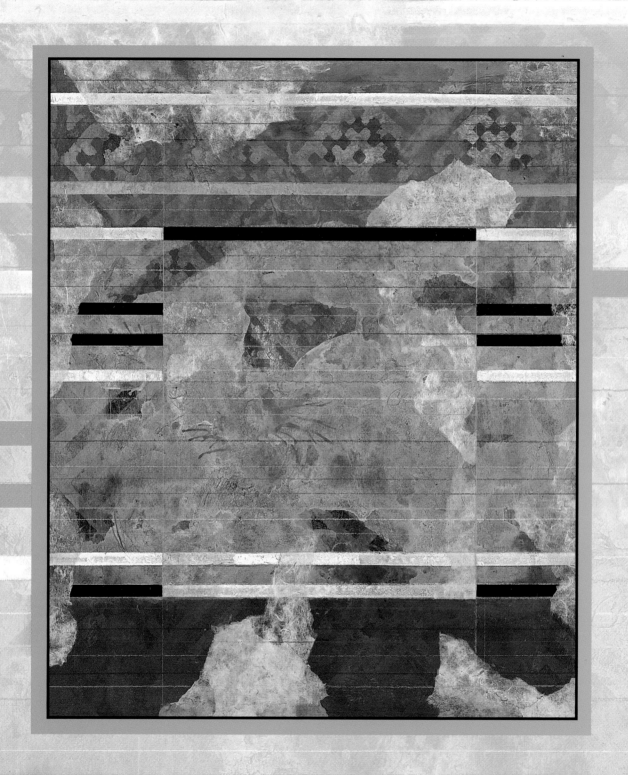

Collagraphy

Collagraphy, the process of making a print from a collage plate, has developed from traditional printmaking methods and the discipline of collage. Although a collage is assembled in the usual manner, it is not the end result; instead, the collage serves as a plate that transfers its textures, shapes, and lines (which must be expressed in relief) to a sheet of paper by means of a printing press. The end result is a two-dimensional work on paper.

The whole range of collage materials that impart texture and dimension—shoestrings, Mylar cutouts, textured fabrics, stalks of wheat, masking tape, scraps of lace, corrugated cardboard, twine, sandpaper, loofah fibers, lengths of macramé, leaves, sequins, tiny pebbles, paper doilies, feathers, crushed eggshells, twigs, and so on—may be affixed to a base (though certain techniques unique to this medium must be employed) to create the evocative juxtapositions and exploration of diverse materials and themes that characterize collage.

Robert Kelly
Kairos V
Collograph
39" x 32" (99 cm x 81 cm)

Jennifer Berringer
In the Balance
Monoprint
32" x 40" (81 cm x 102 cm)

A plate and press can be used to produce a single image or a series of impressions of that image; however, in collagraphy it is sometimes difficult to produce a number of impressions from one plate, because some collage elements may become flattened or distorted after the first impression.

A collagraph's main elements include composition, color, and texture. Its composition is determined by the arrangement of collage elements; its colors result from the selection and application of printing inks or paints to the collage plate; its visual textures reflect those of the particular collage elements. Some artists embellish their prints with glued-on details such as bits of paper and artwork, threads, and wires; others enhance them with hand-rendered touches in paint, colored pencils, or other media.

Collagraphy requires more equipment than other forms of collage, but still constitutes an approachable and pleasantly

Deborah Putnoi
the J in my life
Monoprint
18" x 24" (46 cm x 61 cm)

experimental, improvisational way of creating art. Though primarily a fine art, collagraphy can also be used to create beautiful functional items such as greeting cards, book covers, posters, and illustrations.

Although both are printmakers, the two artists represented in this chapter differ in their approaches to creating collagraphs. Jennifer Berringer employs traditional printmaking techniques to execute her subtle, large-scale collagraphic images. Deborah Putnoi's approach is anything but traditional—her create-as-you-go style results in bold prints alive with spontaneity.

Collagraphy

MATERIALS

To create a collagraph, you will need special

materials and equipment, including a base, collage elements, glue, inks or paints, papers, brayers and brushes, and a printing press or other means to transfer the image from the collage plate to the paper.

First, select a base for the collage elements; the elements will be glued to it to form the plate. If a hand-printing technique will be used instead of a press, you have great freedom in choosing the base—corrugated cardboard, mat board, and even cardboard from shirt packaging are all suitable. If a press is to be used, you will need a much sturdier backing, such as Masonite, canvas board, a metal sheet, Plexiglas, linoleum, or plywood; the base's maximum thickness should be $1/8$ inch (it will be easier to run it through the press if its edges are beveled; you can sand the edges to achieve this). Also, consider the size of the press when deciding on the dimensions of the base.

Next, choose the elements of the collage. Remember that texture and raised (or recessed) patterns will be transferred to the print, but shapes that are not defined in relief will not show up. Also, an item's thickness and porosity must be considered. Elements that are thicker than $1/16$ of an inch will be difficult to print, though you might make an impression of a thick item, such as a jar cap or a door hinge, with modeling paste; it will pass more easily through a printing press and will create a faithful image of the original item. Porous items, such as fabrics and papers, must be treated to make them nonporous, or they will absorb ink and simply print a blurry splotch that lacks the definition and texture of the collage element. Applying a solution of acrylic medium and water will accomplish this.

To secure the collage elements onto the base, you will need a glue that both bonds well with a particular element and will remain strong yet flexible in the printing process. Acrylic gel and PVC glues such as Elmer's Glue-All and Sobo Premium Craft & Fabric Glue will affix cardboard, paper, and cloth successfully.

Emily Myerow
Pear Woman (Spring)
Monotype collage
14" x 18" (36 cm x 46 cm)

Rubber, metal, and wood need special fixatives such as epoxy resins, superglues, and wood glue.

Once the collage plate has been constructed, choose the ink or paint (oils, acrylics, and watercolors are all suitable). Each medium offers a different effect. Water-based paints and inks are easier to clean up because they do not require the use of a solvent. However, printing inks and oil paints offer greater permanence and reliability. (Although oil paints were once preferred over acrylics because of their quality of color, recent advances in the manufacture of acrylic paints have made this judgment obsolete.) Choose a paint or ink according to

the look you want for a particular collagraph. A given work can combine many colors or concentrate on a single hue.

Brayers (hand-held rollers used to apply the ink or paint to the collage plate) are made of hard or soft rubber, plastic, or gelatin, and they range in size from 1¹/₂ inches to 3 inches (3.8 cm to 7.6 cm) in diameter, and up to 2 feet (61 cm) in roller length (though for most projects, rollers of 4 to 6 inches (10.2 cm to 15.2 cm) in length will suffice). The hardness or softness of the roller will affect the application of color—a hard roller will coat only the uppermost surfaces of the collage plate, whereas a soft roller will push the ink into crevices and

depressions. Some printmakers use the end of a tightly rolled length of felt to daub color onto the plate; when the end becomes overused, it can be cut off, bringing fresh felt to the surface. Paintbrushes are not required in the printmaking process, but they can be helpful in applying details. You may also need to wipe excess ink from the plate—cheesecloth, newspaper, or a block of wood can be employed to create different effects.

Although several kinds of paper can be used to make a collagraph, printmaking papers such as Arches and Rives are the best choices. Manufactured specifically for printmaking, they are absorbent and

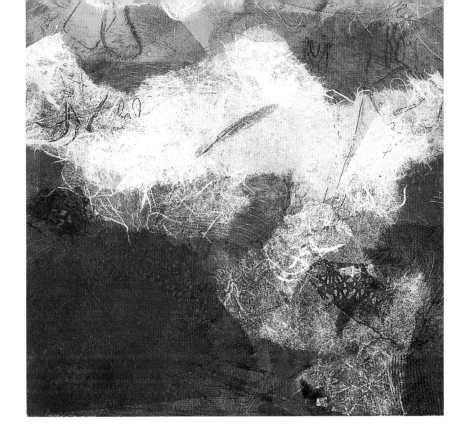

Debra L. Arter
Flight Over
Collagraphy with *chine collé*
9.5" x 9.5" (24 cm x 24 cm)

resist tearing. In general, papers with a high rag content will withstand the printing process well and won't discolor or disintegrate over time. Make sure to cut the paper with ample margins—they should be at least 2 inches (5 cm) larger than the plate at each side. The paper should also fit the press easily. Remember that the paper must usually be dampened before printing can begin.

If you do not have access to a press and wish to create a collagraph by hand, you will need a baren. This rubbing tool is a round disk, 5½ inches (13.4 cm) in diameter. Traditional barens are handmade of many layers of paper bound in bamboo in Japan, where they are used in making woodblock prints; less expensive manufactured models are available in art supply stores.

The other option is to use an etching press to print your collagraph. The inked collage plate, covered with the printing paper and padded with felt printing blankets, is run between the press rollers at high pressure. The paper is thus pushed into the hollows of the plate to absorb ink and be imprinted with texture. The result is a completed collagraph, ready for drying and then displaying.

Collagraphy
TECHNIQUES

Once you have assembled the necessary materials

and equipment—a base, collage elements, glues, inks or paints, brayers, brushes, printing paper, and a printing press or barens—you can begin to compose your collagraph. Lay out the collage elements on the base, keeping in mind that the printed image will be reversed. If you have cut letters out of cardboard for text, for example, remember to apply them backward.

Before gluing any pieces into place, consider how the textures will transfer onto the print: a smooth element such as a Mylar sheet will not retain much ink on its surface after wiping, but ink will settle around its edges, thus defining its shape on the print; a string dipped into acrylic gel and placed on the base will create a line; partially raveled fabric (after it has been treated to make it nonporous) will print a fringed edge.

Choose collage elements that are not too thick; it is difficult to ensure a quality print when the paper has to be forced around items thicker than 1/16

inch. You may thin dense plant materials—cut flowers in half, or strip some of the leaves from a stalk (dried plant materials tend to hold their shape better; they must also be treated to make them nonporous). You may also make an impression of a thicker item, such as a key or an acorn—grease the item, coat one side with a paste or cement such as acrylic modeling paste, and then apply it to an absolutely flat sheet of paper (you might tape the paper down to ensure flatness as the paste dries). After several hours have passed, remove the item and cut off the excess paper. You may wish to use fine sandpaper to smooth the impression and reduce thick areas. Use the impression as you would any other collage element.

Next, treat any porous elements (paper, fabric, plant materials) to prevent them from absorbing ink. A thin application (on both sides) using a solution of water and acrylic medium will seal out moisture, allowing the surface to be coated with ink that will transfer its texture to the print. (Untreated material would absorb the ink like a sponge, printing an undefined blotch of color.) It is also possible to seal these elements after they have been glued to the base—just make sure the seal is complete.

Glue each collage element to the base, using glues that suit each material. You may also texture the base itself by cutting into it or by applying gesso or gels mixed with other materials (such as sand or crushed eggshells). After each element is glued into place, let the completed plate dry thoroughly. Clean off any nubs or thick streaks of glue or gel; otherwise they will show up on the print.

Next, prepare the colors. Though you may also use a brush or dauber to apply inks, a brayer is most typically used. Squeeze the colors onto a smooth palette, such as a Plexiglas sheet, to ensure that the brayer will be evenly coated. Tailor your choice of brayer and amount of ink to create the effect you desire. If you want all the surfaces of a built-up area to be inked, use a brayer with a soft roller and a liberal application of color. If you want only the topmost parts to print, use a brayer with a hard roller and less color. Textured surfaces that are left uncolored will emboss the paper as it rolls through the press; however, take care to protect these areas and other white spaces from trickles of ink. Wear cotton or plastic gloves to keep your hands clean.

For smooth, even color, inked areas should be wiped after the color is applied. Wiping with a cheesecloth produces a mottled effect that can help in blending colors. To effect a greater contrast between recessed and built-up sections of the plate, wipe with even strokes, using pieces of newsprint or even a block of wood; this removes ink from the top surfaces, yet leaves more in crevices and folds. You may need to repeat this process once or twice to distribute the ink or paint evenly. If, however, the color has been applied in a unique fashion, perhaps with brushes or in patterns not intended to cover a whole area, wiping may not be necessary.

Before printing, the paper must be cut to the correct size (leave at least a 2-inch margin on each side of the plate) and then dampened. This step removes sizing in the paper and softens it so that it can receive the imprint of the collage elements. Some papers must be soaked in a tray of water for a few hours; unsized papers may only need to be dipped quickly. Prepare the paper in advance, so that it is damp but not soaking wet at the time you will be ready to print. Handle the paper gently; it will be stronger after it has dried completely, but it can easily be torn when wet.

To prepare for printing, cover the inked plate with the paper, aligning it carefully so that there are even margins on each side (or you may prefer a wider margin on the bottom edge). Cover the paper with two or three felt printing blankets, which protect the paper as it passes through the press. You may wish to add foam padding to built-up areas on the plate to help it move smoothly through the press. It might be necessary to place a thin sheet of plastic between the paper and the blankets to protect them from glue or excess moisture. Then carefully run the print through the press. Some collagraph artists run a few proofs to fine-tune color, composition, and pressure.

You may instead use a baren to transfer the image to the paper. After placing the paper over the plate, rub the paper with the padded portion of the baren to obtain a smoothly transferred image. Using the edge of the baren will give a sharper outline. You can vary the pressure to create a range of effects.

Handle the completed print carefully. You may wish to touch up some details with color before drying the print. To dry it, sandwich it between several sheets of blotting paper, place these papers between sheets of newsprint, and then place all the papers between boards. Weight the boards with books or bricks, so that the print will dry flat, and replace the sheets of newsprint as they become wet. Keep the print weighted until it is entirely dry; then embellish it with lead or colored pencils, if you wish.

It is sometimes possible to create more than one print from a single collagraph plate. However, if the plate contains fragile items such as plant materials and tissue papers, subsequent printings may be unsuccessful. Plates made of more durable materials may be re-inked immediately after the first print is pulled, and then printed again. If you would like to print at a later date, clean the plate carefully (use solvents if oil-based colors were used, and water for water-based colors). Make sure that the cleaning agent will not destroy the glue bond.

Because of the many variables involved in making collagraph prints, experimentation and experience play important roles in the process. Expect surprises! Read up on the subject, refine your technique, and then let inspiration guide you.

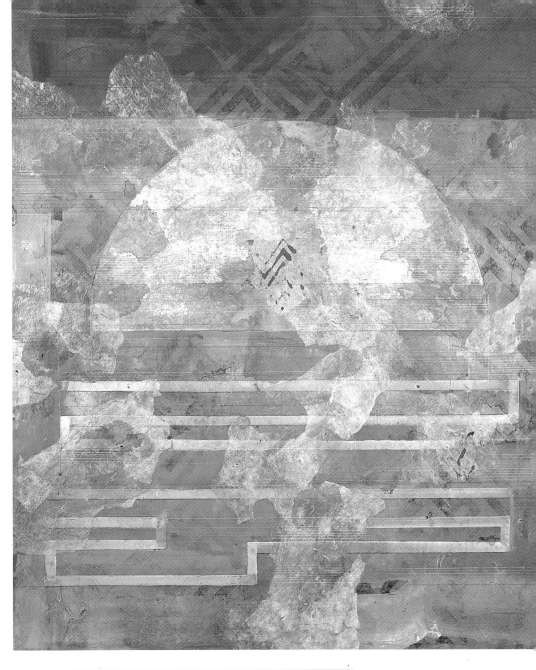

Robert Kelly
Ghanto XII
Collagraphy with mixed media
54" x 42" (137 cm x 107 cm)

Meryl Brater
The Belly of Stones
Collagraphy with drawing in
mixed media book
(detail)

JENNIFER BERRINGER

ACCIDENTAL
Music

Jennifer Berringer's prints combine both formal

and organic elements in large-scale, expressive abstractions. The scale she works in has grown beyond the dimensions of her press, and she often assembles panels in diptychs and triptychs.

The square and rectangular shapes that predominate in her prints are punctuated with bits of glued paper, threads and strings, metal strips, sequins, and swatches of fabric. Together with the lines, squiggles, and spirals that she scratches into areas of ink, these details bring a sense of intimacy and animation to her work. As she builds up collage elements on the base, Berringer emphasizes the natural properties of paper—crinkled areas, torn edges, and layered effects subtly texture her prints. Her palette features muted tones of beige and gray, though she somtimes adds brighter colors for contrast.

Berringer employs traditional techniques in creating, sealing, and inking a plate for printing, but she is not interested in exercising complete control over the process: she enjoys the experimental aspect of the work, which she likens to laying down riffs in jazz. She often makes several proofs of a print, varying the application of ink (wiped smooth with cheesecloth or brushed on more heavily, for example) and the pressure of the press until she is satisfied with the result. Berringer appreciates the unpredictable nature of the medium, often finding that an unexpected effect enhances her work.

Dream Journal IV
Collagraph
62" x 82" (157 cm x 208 cm)

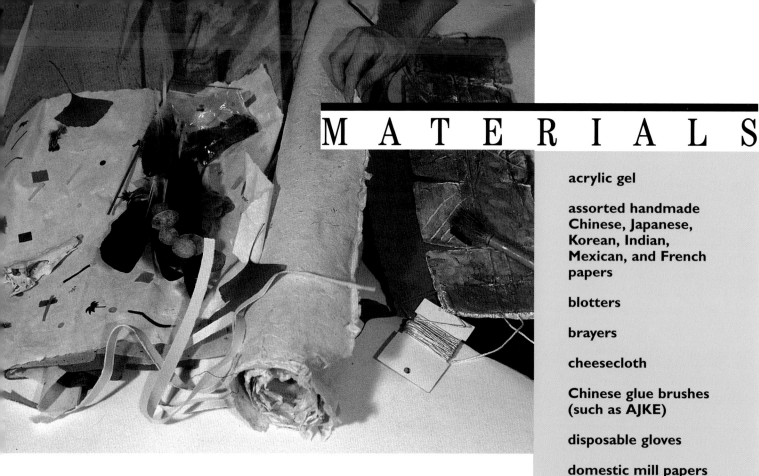

MATERIALS

The artist begins to plan her collagraphic plate by choosing from the materials she has collected: paper, scraps of wire and fabric, and leftover pieces of her artwork.

All That's Fit to Print

In addition to many kinds of paper (bits of sheet music, crepe paper, crumpled tissue), you may also affix ribbons, metal foil, and fabrics by placing them on the base facedown, with the glue side up. Small pieces work best.

acrylic gel

assorted handmade Chinese, Japanese, Korean, Indian, Mexican, and French papers

blotters

brayers

cheesecloth

Chinese glue brushes (such as AJKE)

disposable gloves

domestic mill papers (such as Carriage House, Rugg Road)

etching ink in a variety of colors

etching press

gesso

mat board for base

metal wire

printmaking paper (such as Rives BFK)

PVA glue (such as Elmer's Glue-All)

sharp tools for scratching into the inked plate

string

1 Berringer lays out pieces of paper and string on the collagraphic base, a large piece of mat board.

2 Berringer plans to attach these papers to the print's surface by applying glue to them and then placing them on the base, glue side up (this method of affixing papers is called chine collé). They will adhere to the print paper as it runs through the press.

3 Berringer applies a thin coating of PVA glue to a delicate paper, which will form part of the print's surface.

4 The artist attaches the selected materials to the collagraphic plate with gesso.

5 Here Berringer seals the plate, first using gesso and then an application of acrylic gel medium for an even finish. This treatment prevents the fabric and paper elements from absorbing ink like a sponge, which would then result in a messy blur when run through the press. The acrylic coating will allow the ink to pool in the crevices, lines, and indentations that define each element's surface, thus reproducing each item's unique texture in the collagraph print.

6 After mixing the colors, the artist begins to ink the plate. She uses a number of tools to apply the ink, including brayers, brushes, squeegees, tarlatan (a stiff cloth), and even her hands; here, she uses a piece of cheesecloth. Berringer wipes some areas after applying ink, to lighten the color or to smooth the application. Sometimes she works back and forth between applying and wiping, building up colors in some areas and lightening or blending them in others.

7 Sometimes the artist scratches designs into the wet ink.

8 Here the artist rolls the dampened sheet of printmaking paper over the plate, which combines inked collage elements and pieces that will be glued onto the print's surface. After the felt-printing blankets are placed over the paper, the printing process can begin. The scale of Berringer's prints requires a press with a 48-by-84-inch bed.

9 The artist checks the printed image at the press, to ensure that the applied papers have bonded well. She will re-glue any loose pieces. It is preferable to do re-gluing at this stage, rather than to apply too much glue to the papers before printing—since the glue may seep through the paper onto the felt blankets.

10 To dry the piece, Berringer places it between tissue papers and blotters; then it is pressed between boards for several days until it is dry.

11 After the drying is complete, Berringer enhances the print with pastels, graphite, and oil crayon.

DEBORAH PUTNOI

COLLECTIVE Memory

Deborah Putnoi's world reflects her interest

in the themes of community and the way that collective memory is transmitted from generation to generation. She often employs imagery from everyday life, such as the human figure, domestic animals, playing children, and food. A sense of continuing dialogue is present in her work because of her frequent use of text and letters, her incorporation of pieces of her old work and old drypoint plates, and the way that one piece often suggests the themes of following works.

Putnoi rarely plans her pieces in advance. She works spontaneously, combining cutout shapes, applied papers, figures scratched into areas of paint, and ink drawings. She revises her work as she goes along, rearranging elements, drawing or painting over images, and trimming cut pieces to refine their shapes. She skips some of the traditional, methodical techniques of printmaking, such as sealing the plate and wiping areas of ink into place; instead, she prefers to work quickly and instinctively, allowing the random effects of the printing process to lend immediacy to her work. Putnoi's output is prolific, and she keeps a visual journal to provide inspiration and to generate new ideas.

Green apple + T
Monoprint
11" x 15" (28 cm x 38 cm)

MATERIALS

Putnoi uses a variety of materials in making her prints—her own used drypoint plates, remnants of her prints, cardboard cutouts, cloth, twist ties, flattened bottle caps—any odds and ends that are interesting in shape and texture.

assorted fabrics and papers

bamboo ink brush

blotter paper

brayers in different sizes

disposable gloves

etched aluminum drypoint plate

etching press

etching tools

X-Acto knife

Japanese calligraphy ink

mineral oil

oil paint in a variety of colors

paintbrushes

paper (such as Stonehenge)

palette knife

Plexiglas base

Plexiglas palette

PVA glue (such as Sobo Premium Craft & Fabric Glue)

scissors

thin cardboard with a finished side (such as Bristol board)

After she chooses her collage materials, Putnoi begins to lay out her palette. She mixes oil paints with a palette knife on a Plexiglas palette, which she can wipe off easily and reuse.

Using a brayer, the artist applies paint to the sheet of Plexiglas that will serve as the base for the plate. She continues to mix and alter her paint palette throughout the process of preparing the plate. The disposable cloth gloves help keep the paper clean.

At this stage, Putnoi draws into an inked area of the base with the end of a paintbrush. She also applies cutout collage elements, inking them before placing them on the base. An old drypoint plate has been freshly inked to transfer its image to the paper as well.

4 Putnoi often glues collage elements directly onto the clean printing paper prior to running it through the press. Here she is creating such a piece, using Japanese calligraphy ink and a bamboo brush. When this piece has dried, it will be glued onto the printing paper.

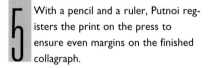

5 With a pencil and a ruler, Putnoi registers the print on the press to ensure even margins on the finished collagraph.

6 In the final step before printing, the artist has selected a piece of an old print to apply facedown on the plate. Glue on the side facing up will affix the piece to the printing paper as it passes through the press.

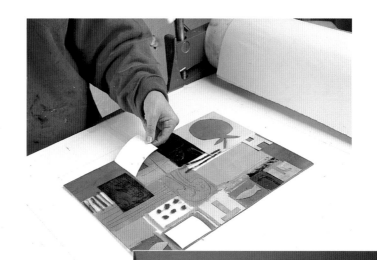

7 Putnoi runs the print through the press. In order for the image to transfer clearly, she has to run it through more than once.

Wet/Dry Technique

You might experiment with using both wet and dry paper for printing your collagraph, as Putnoi does. Dry paper can work well, provided that the collage elements are quite flat; a wet paper will absorb more ink and receive a clearer impression of textures and relief.

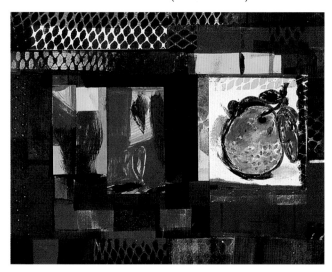

▲ **Diane Miller**
Noon Waterfall
Monotype collage
25" x 19" (64 cm x 48 cm)

GALLERY

▲ **Emily Myerow**
Chinese Take-Out #1
Monotype collage
14" x 18" (36 cm x 46 cm)

▼ Diane Miller
Waterfall IX
Monotype collage
25" x 19" (64 cm x 48 cm)

◄ Betty Guernsey
Old Fashioned Garden
Mixed media monoprint
30" x 20" (76 cm x 51 cm)

© Betty Guernsey, New York City

▲ Betty Guernsey
Jubilee
Mixed media monoprint
30" x 20" (76 cm x 51 cm)

© Betty Guernsey, New York City

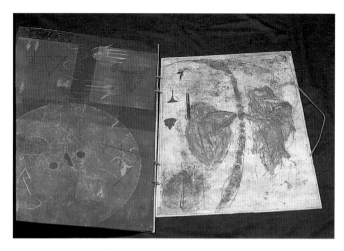

◀ **Meryl Brater**
Pugillaris
Collagraph
28.5" x 90" (72 cm x 229 cm)
(detail, left)

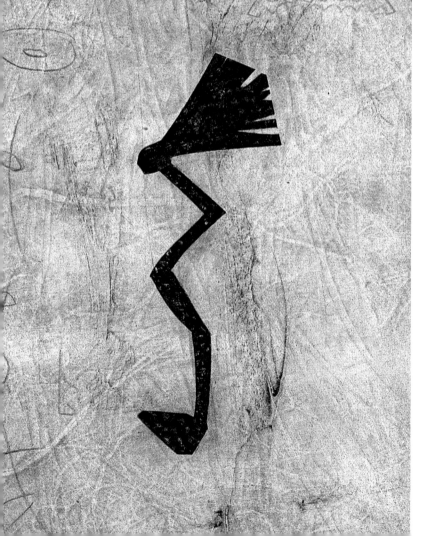

▲ **Debra L. Arter**
Thoughts on Flight II
Collagraphy with unryu paper, stencil
resist, and *chine collé*
9.5" x 9.5" (24 cm x 24 cm)

◀ **Meryl Brater**
The Form of Language Book II
Collagraphy with drawing
8.5" x 6.5" (22 cm x 17 cm)

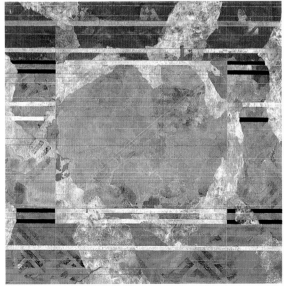

Robert Kelly ▶
Suttra Series
Collagraphy with mixed media
26" x 36" (66 cm x 91 cm)

▼ Debra L. Arter
Violet Tidal View II
Collagraphy with *chine collé*
8" x 6" (20 cm x 15 cm)

▲ Robert Kelly
Kairos III
Collagraphy with mixed media
50" x 45" (127 cm x 114 cm)

◀ **Jennifer Berringer**
Roma
Collagraph
28" x 40" (71 cm x 102 cm)

Jennifer Berringer ▶
Polydore
Collagraph
60" x 80" (152 cm x 203 cm)

Deborah Putnoi ▶
and when we
Monoprint
12" x 30" (30 cm x 76 cm)

◀ **Deborah Putnoi**
For Both
Monoprint
18" x 24" (46 cm x 61 cm)

Found Object

COLLAGE

Found object collage (sometimes called assemblage) draws two- and three-dimensional objects from everyday life, both organic and man-made, into the realm of art. The associations we attach to particular items and the way they are juxtaposed may evoke a sense of harmony or dissonance, serenity or turmoil, unity or disarray. This form of collage is now in its heyday because of the contemporary interest in recycling, the nostalgia for mass-produced icons of pop culture (such as Mickey Mouse watches, buttons from presidential campaigns of the past, outdated kitchen appliances, and mood rings), and the twentieth century's broadened definition of the materials and themes that can constitute art. Yet, in addition to its role as a fine art medium, found object collage may be used to decorate many domestic items, such as frames and boxes.

Carole P. Kunstadt
Memories
Collage with mixed media
4" x 6" (10 cm x 15 cm)
Mark Karlsberg

▲ **Frances Hamilton**
Angel
Collage with gouache
9.5" x 11.5" (24 cm x 29 cm)

◄ **Frances Hamilton**
Going Home
Collage with gouache
16.5" x 25" (42 cm x 64 cm)

Creating this type of collage involves securing found objects to a base. Glue, nails, hooks, or other means may be used. The objects themselves may be enhanced with paint or distressed to lend the effect of aging. The rules for creating found objects collage are few, and they involve practical considerations, such as choosing fasteners that will firmly support the objects.

This chapter's featured artists use found objects in different ways. Douglas Bell employs them as collage elements in his abstract paintings. Ben Freeman makes found objects the focus of his work, beginning each collage by creating a sketch and choosing pieces that will mesh together to suggest a narrative. Both artists, like Joseph Cornell, look beyond an item's original purpose, reinterpreting it and endowing it with new meaning.

Nancy Rubens
One's Own Time
16" x 12" (41 cm x 30 cm)

Found Object

MATERIALS

For most collages employing three-dimensional

items, a sturdy foundation such as plywood, mat board, multidensity fiberboard, Masonite, or cardboard should be selected as a base. Each option has benefits and drawbacks. Plywood is strong, inexpensive, and easy to find, but it can warp. Multidensity fiberboard, which is made from compressed wood pulp, does not warp and is also inexpensive, but it is heavy and thus can be awkward to work with. Masonite is less porous than wood and will not warp, but it costs more and can be hard to find. Mat board is lightweight and sturdy, comes in many colors, and is acid-free and therefore relatively permanent; however, it is too thin to support all but the lightest found objects. Cardboard, the least expensive and most readily available base, is less sturdy and less permanent than the other possible choices.

You could also use a found object as a base, provided that it is strong and stable enough to support the other objects. An old kitchen cabinet door, a shallow crate, a large cutting board, even an old Beatles' album jacket—or the vinyl record itself—could serve as the foundation for the collage. When you attach the other objects, choose a fixative that will not harm the found object base.

Fasteners must be strong enough to permanently support the weight of a given object. For heavy items, staple guns can be handy to use, but the staples tend to stand out, and an object might be marred by them. Screws and nails can attach an object firmly, and the heads can be covered with wood putty or another material, making them invisible in the finished collage.

Ellen Wineberg
Thanatos
Monotype collage with woodcut on paper
27" x 26" (69 cm x 66 cm)

Or you might prefer to leave such hardware visible, making it an integral part of the collage; consider using weathered nails, colored tacks, or decorative brackets. Eccentric choices such as clamps, metal chain, roping, or hooks might suit certain collages.

To attach papers, fabrics, and other lightweight items, use a glue that will bond the material to the base successfully. Acrylic gel is a good adhesive for papers and fabrics; once it dries, it will be transparent and colorless. Gesso (white acrylic polymer) also works well on paper, fabric, mat board, and Masonite. You can also use it to create texture on the surface of the base. Rubber cement affixes paper smoothly, but note that the paper can also be peeled off again—the bond is not permanent. Water-soluble PVA glues such as Elmer's Glue-All and Sobo Premium Craft & Fabric Glue are convenient for gluing fabric and paper.

Items made of wood, glass, plastic, and metal require other fixatives. You might choose Elmer's Wood Glue to attach wooden objects to the base. Silicone adhesive works well on glass and metal. Epoxy resins will secure plastics and metals; they can be purchased in hardware stores in a variety of forms. They produce a strong, permanent bond but are toxic—observe the directions and warnings on the label. Superglues also provide a permanent bond for many materials, but they too are toxic and must be used with care.

After all the objects are affixed, allow the piece to dry thoroughly. Check that each item is bonded securely before displaying your finished work.

Peter Madden
Sinister Nature
Collage transfers on cotton, copper, brass, wood
30.5" x 39" (77 cm x 99 cm)

Found Object
TECHNIQUES

To begin a found object collage, gather a variety

of objects such as cigar boxes, seashells, broken crockery, old photos, buttons, small baskets, driftwood, scraps of metal, sea glass, game pieces, an old calendar, playing cards, a baseball cap, dice—whatever strikes your fancy. Don't forget to consider bits and pieces of your old artwork that might suit your theme. Found objects can be composed on a flat surface or arranged in boxes or other containers. You might group souvenirs from a favorite holiday or gather mementos from a significant year in your life; or you may mix seemingly disparate objects that evoke a theme or have a subtle relationship.

Once you have collected your objects, decide on the base for your collage. Plywood will successfully support heavy objects; mat board or canvas will serve well for very light objects. You may wish to treat the base with paint (anything from a wash to a detailed painting) or to texture it with gesso before applying the found objects. Rearrange the pieces on the base until you are satisfied with the composition.

You can also enhance the individual objects of the collage in a number of ways, both to create interesting effects and to stabilize fragile elements. Paper and fabric items can be torn, twisted, shredded, or folded; heavier objects can be distressed by scratching, sanding, or nicking; a variety of elements can be stenciled or written on. You can apply a backing to fragile fabrics to help them hold their shape. Dip dry flowers or leaves in acrylic medium to preserve color and shape.

After the individual elements and the layout of the collage are in order, the practical considerations of assembling the work take over.

How will you attach the objects to the base? Decide which pieces should be fastened with glue and which will need stronger support. Generally, papers, fabrics, and lightweight objects can be affixed with glue; choose a glue that suits each material. You may need to experiment with various glues and the amount to apply to ensure a firm bond.

Heavier objects will need to be attached with hardware. Nails, screws, or hooks can work well. Tailor the size of the hardware to the thickness of the base—a nail that is too large will split a thin board. Experiment, or ask a knowledgeable assistant at the hardware store to help you select the best hardware for your purposes.

Douglas Bell
Untitled
Collage with acrylic and mixed media on paper
30" x 22" (76 cm x 56 cm)

Attach the collage elements in a logical sequence. For instance, if a large horseshoe is to be nailed in place next to a fragile bunch of dried flowers, apply the horseshoe first to prevent damaging the flowers with the pounding of the hammer. Consider applying the largest objects first, followed by the smaller details. Let glued areas dry thoroughly, and check that each object is fixed securely.

Once all the pieces are attached to the base, a few finishing touches may be in order. You might add painted details, cover nailheads with putty, apply subtle finishes such as glitter or spattered paint to parts of the collage, or sand rough areas to put a final polish on your work.

William Harrington
Art as Therapy
Collage with mixed media
10" x 12" (25 cm x 30 cm)

Ellen Wineberg
Cardinal
Collage with pastel on paper
16" x 20" (41 cm x 51 cm)
Photo by David Caras

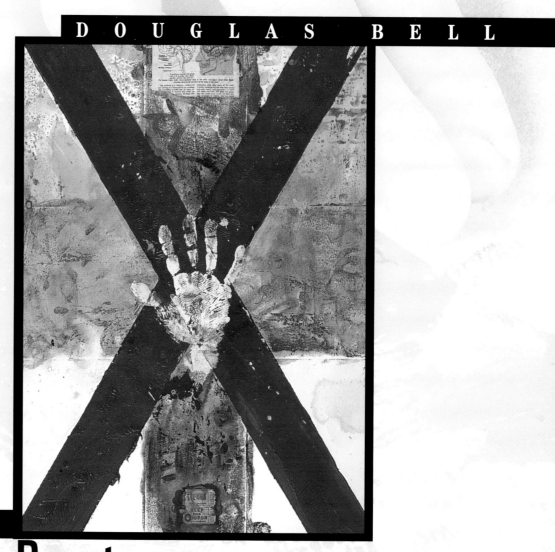

DOUGLAS BELL

OBJECTS
With a Past

When he works with found objects, Douglas

tries to recapture the thrill of making things that he felt as a child. His two- and three-dimensional paintings incorporate found objects imbued with an archaeological feeling, as if they have been rediscovered and given a new incarnation in his artwork. He often uses worn objects, or distresses the surfaces of newer ones, so that they evoke the past. Though the viewer may recognize something familiar in the items he uses, his presentation of an object-removed from its typical context, surrounded with other images, and perhaps layered with paint or other materials-gives it a sense of mystery.

Bell's use of materials stems from an artistic frugality; he makes do with the materials at hand and likes to fix and save things for future use. He employs trimmings from unfinished paintings and drawings, building personal history and a sense of continuity into his works. His unusual ways of using paint—daubing it onto boards or papers, and then applying it to his work—add interesting textures.

Certain themes recur in Bell's work. He is particularly interested in the way numbers and letters can represent superstitions, symbolic meanings, the uncertainties of chance and gambling, mystery, and a means of control. Bell also explores the human tendency to apply systems to random events in order to organize and understand life.

Red X with Tickets
Paper and found object collage with oil paint
30" x 22" (76 cm x 56 cm)

MATERIALS

- acrylic paints

- assorted collage materials, including tickets

- board for applying paint

- brayer

- extra-heavy acrylic gel

- paintbrushes in various sizes

- palette knife

- paper for base (such as Rives BFK)

- sandpaper

- scraps of paper

- squeegees

- water

Bell collects boxes of surplus objects (especially similar items in multiples), tickets, wooden wheels, glass bottles, numbered map pins, scraps from various manufacturing processes, and other found objects. Here, he assembles some of the objects, together with pieces of his artwork, to begin composing his collage.

1 Bell applies an acrylic-and-water wash to the base of his collage. This wash is the first of many that he will use to build color on the surface.

2 Bell decides on the placement of the collage elements. He will affix them with gel medium and a small paintbrush on the paper base.

Wash and Dry Tip
Between steps, let washes and acrylic gel dry completely, to ensure clear colors and the successful completion of the next step.

3 To create surface texture, Bell uses a palette knife to add a layer of gel medium over the entire base.

4 At this point, Bell covers certain areas of the collage with scrap paper so that they will remain white. He then daubs paint onto another piece of paper, which he places facedown on a section of the base. After applying pressure with a brayer, he slowly peels back the paper to reveal a stippled pattern of paint.

Save the Scraps

Save the pieces of paper used to apply paint in this way. They often have interesting patterns that might be useful in your next project.

5 Bell uses a number of unorthodox techniques to add color to his collages. For this piece, he applies red paint to a two-by-four, which he then places facedown on the collage (the collage has been placed on a drop cloth). He walks on the board to apply pressure.

6 The artist adds a handprint to the center of the painted X by coating his palm with white acrylic paint.

7 For the final step, Bell sands the surface of the painting to impart a distressed appearance to the work. He also uses the sandpaper to smooth papers that were torn a bit during the application of paint.

BEN FREEMAN

SCRAPBOOK
Images

Ben Freeman's work expresses his nostalgia

for the past while creating a reference point for the present. In his collages, studded with old photographs and architectural elements, he employs images that seem familiar—perhaps similar to those in the viewer's old photograph albums at home. But the mysterious people and places in these photographs are also strangers whom we want to know, to fit into a narrative suggested by the found objects surrounding them. Thus Freeman takes the viewer into the past while bringing the past into the present.

Freeman has scouted antique stores and flea markets to gather images of intriguing people and evocative places. He begins a collage by choosing a subject from his collection of vintage photographs, often enlarging the image and embellishing it with painted details. He also incorporates into his collages old maps, postcards, journals, and letters—the souvenirs to which people attach memories. These details, though they may provide hints to the viewer concerning the subject's mood, identity, and experience, mainly express the mystery of human life and the ephemeral nature of human experience.

Unfinished Works: Diane
Found objects on wood
36" x 36" (64 cm x 64 cm)

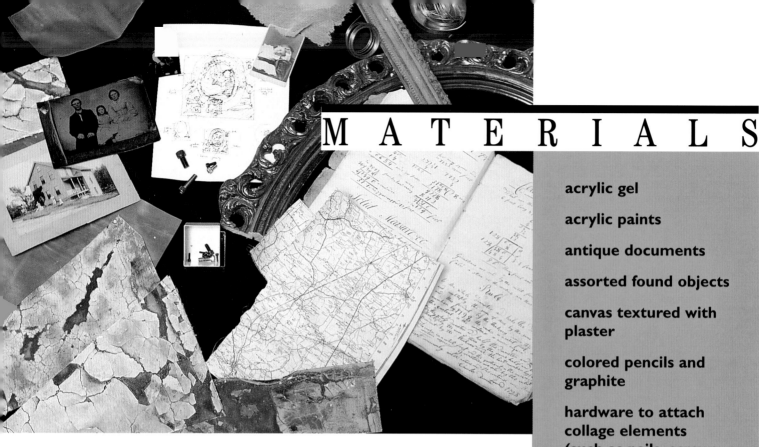

MATERIALS

F reeman decides to focus his found object collage on a tiny photograph of a little girl wearing a melancholy expression. He also makes selections from his stash of old maps, photographs of places, lace and other fabric, parts of vintage frames, architectural elements, writings, and handmade and found papers.

acrylic gel

acrylic paints

antique documents

assorted found objects

canvas textured with plaster

colored pencils and graphite

hardware to attach collage elements (such as nails, screws, and wire)

industrial contact cement

lace and other fabric swatches

lead sheeting

oil stick (such as Winsor Newton)

oil varnishes (such as Winsor Newton Matte)

old photographs

plywood board for base

stretcher bars

1 Freeman has had the photograph of the girl enlarged. Using contact cement, he has glued the enlargement to the plywood base. He applied the cement with a broad brush and then affixed the image to the plywood beginning at one edge, rolling out the photograph smoothly to leave no bubbles under the surface. Now he considers other elements that might complement the photograph.

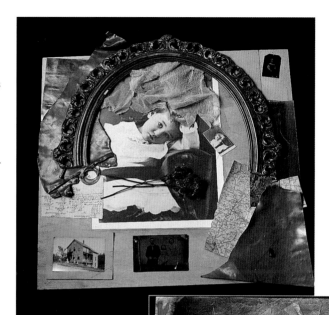

2 Next, Freeman works on enhancing the image with oil paints and graphite.

Using a Glue Brush

Using a broad brush to apply glue helps in making a quick, thorough application; none of the glue will begin to dry before the object is applied to the base, and the even application will help ensure a smooth surface.

3 The artist narrows his choices of collage elements by juxtaposing them with the completed image of the girl. He considers adding fabric details, such as lace to enhance the dress. Freeman then attaches the paper pieces with gel medium and the three-dimensional pieces with contact cement.

4 Now Freeman covers the entire piece with a large square of lead sheeting. The lead is smoothed with a roller to flatten it completely against the plywood surface and then is secured with stretcher bars. Next, the artist begins the process of cutting away certain areas with a mat knife to reveal the collage elements beneath it. He can feel the edges of the photographs beneath the soft lead and thus knows where to cut. (Because of lead's toxicity, dispose of any scraps where children can't reach them.)

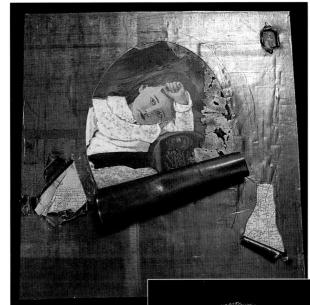

5 Freeman creates a neat, rolled-back edge to set off the photograph of the little girl and the swatch of the map. He uses a crinkled, irregular edge to reveal a part of the handwritten letter and the tiny photograph in the corner.

6 After the cutting of the lead sheet is finished, Freeman considers the placement of collage elements that will be affixed to the surface of the lead sheet. At this stage Freeman begins to apply the other surface objects—a tintype, a photograph, a bunch of dried roses sealed in acrylic medium, a fragment of sheer fabric, and part of an old frame.

▲ **Ben Freeman**
Unfinished Works: Julie
Photograph, found objects on wood
36" x 36" (91 cm x 91 cm)

▲ **Ben Freeman**
Unfinished Works: Claire
Photograph, found objects on wood
36" x 36" (91 cm x 91 cm)

Douglas Bell ▶
Mermaid
Collage with oil, acrylic, and mixed
media on paper
9" x 7" (23 cm x 18 cm)

GALLERY

▲ **Nancy Rubens**
Handle with Care
18" x 14" (46 cm x 36 cm)

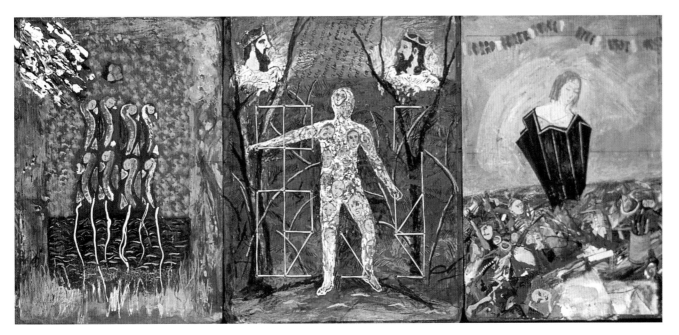

▲ **Francis Hamilton**
Dante
Collage with gouache
11" x 33" (28 cm x 84 cm)

▲ **Francis Hamilton**
Everyday Fun
Collage with gouache, cast paper, wood
17.5" x 24" (44 cm x 61 cm)

◄ **William Harrington**
A Repro
Collage with mixed media
10" x 12" (25 cm x 30 cm)

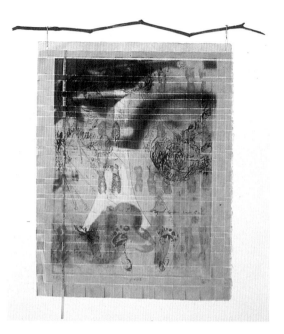

▲ **Lori A. Warner**
Untitled
Solvent transfer on woven oriental paper
8" x 6" (20 cm x 15 cm)

▲ **Ellen Wineberg**
Number 6
Monotype collage with woodcut on wood
28" x 29" (71 cm x 74 cm)

Lori A. Warner ▶
Epigenesis
Solvent transfer with silkscreen intaglio
on woven painted paper
14" x 11" (36 cm x 28 cm)

Janice Fassinger
Loss of Comfort
Collage with painted canvas, photographs, fiber, and beads
25" x 25" (64 cm x 64 cm)

Susan Hass
Ancient Runes
Collage with cyanotype, brownprint, plastic, wire, string, kozo paper, and handmade paper
44" x 29" (112 cm x 74 cm)

Susan Hass ▶
Collective Memory
Collage with alternative photo process
30" x 20" (76 x 51 cm)

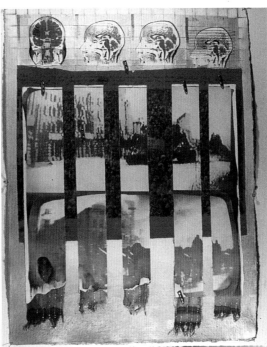

133

▲ **Joyce Yesucevitz**
Remembrance
Collage with acrylic on linen
9" x 21" (23 cm x 53 cm)

▲ **Joyce Yesucevitz**
Cows
Collage with acrylic and burlap on canvas
60" x 48" (152 cm x 122 cm)

▲ **Carole P. Kunstadt**
Funghi
Collage with mixed media
6" x 12" (15 cm x 30 cm)
Photo by Robert Kunstadt

▲ **Carole P. Kunstadt**
Above Treeline
Collage with mixed media
8" x 6" (15 cm x 20 cm)
Photo by Robert Kunstadt

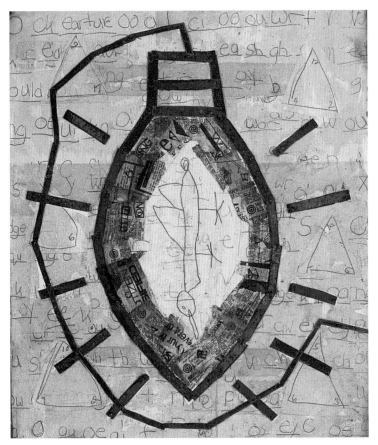

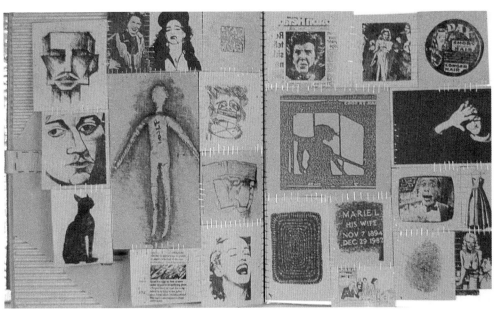

▲ **Dawn Southworth**
Untitled
Collage with mixed media
18" x 15" (46 cm x 38 cm)

◄ **Dawn Southworth**
Untitled
Collage with mixed media
18" x 15" (46 cm x 38 cm)

Peter Madden ►
Biography
Collage transfers on cardboard
18" x 24" (46 cm x 61 cm)

Douglas Bell
97 Walk Hill Street
Jamaica Plain, MA 02130
617-522-7068
or:
c/o Clark Gallery
P. O. Box 339
Lincoln, MA 01773
617-259-8303
617-259-8314 fax

◄ **Douglas Bell**
IOU
Collage with acrylic and mixed media
on canvas
12" x 12" (30 cm x 30 cm)

Doug Bell has spent most of his adult life as an artist trying to recapture "the thrill of making things" he felt growing up in Smithfield, Rhode Island. As a child, he built model kits and customized them with scraps in his basement workshop. As a young man, Bell considered channeling his creativity into a career as an architect or engineer. Although he had a number of artistic interests, including choral singing and painting "sets" for the theater, he realized in college that his true calling was to become an artist.

Bell majored in sculpture at Rhode Island College, and, upon graduating, became a member of the cooperative Bromfield Gallery in Boston, Massachusetts. In 1986, he began exhibiting his work at the Clark Gallery, Lincoln, Massachusetts, and has since been featured in many one-man and group shows.

Jennifer Berringer
9300 Pine View Lane
Clinton, MD 20735
or:
c/o Clark Gallery
P. O. Box 339
145 Lincoln Road
Lincoln, MA 01773

▼ **Jennifer Berringer**
Kinship
48" x 64" (122 cm x 163 cm)

Jennifer Berringer received her degree in art and religion from Montclair State University in 1972 and has been working as an artist since. Berringer lived in Boston, Massachusetts from 1978 through the early 1980s, a prolific period she describes by saying, "At that stage in my life, I was fortunate to have a lot of time to make artwork." A year in Denmark convinced her to apply her talents exclusively to her art and to aggressively pursue an art career. As she states, "As you learn techniques, you make images and spend time building a visual vocabulary. I was looking for a medium to express what I wanted to say. After some early experiments with wax painting, she settled on the medium of collography in 1978.

Sandra Donabed

130 Washington Street
Wellesley, MA 02181
617-237-6390

Sandra Donabed grew up in Buffalo, New York, the daughter of a home economics teacher. She made doll clothes as a child and her own clothes as a young woman. After completing a degree in design at Syracuse University, she moved to Boston, received an education degree from the Massachusetts College of Art, and began teaching high school art in Wellesley, Massachusetts. Donabed's interest in quilting began in the early 1980s, when she joined a class that focused on traditional handwork.

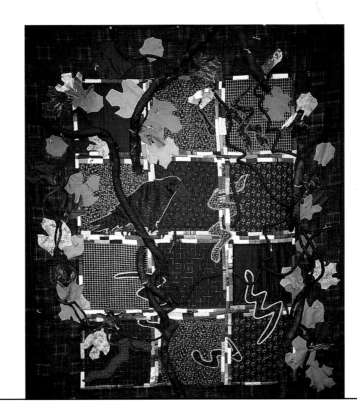

◀ **Sandra Donabed**
Fireflies
45" x 54" (114 cm x 137 cm)

Ben Freeman

300 Summer Street
Boston, MA 02116
617-482-1721
or:
c/o Barbara Krakow Gallery
10 Newbury Street
Boston, MA 02116

Ben Freeman received his degree in architecture in 1969, from the University of North Carolina. He moved to Cambridge, Massachusetts, where he received a Harvard fellowship to study in the Paris office of Le Corbusier. He later did graphic design for French television, where he met and became friends with other artists. These influences lead Freeman to begin painting. He returned to the United States in 1972, with the intention of practicing architecture for a short time before returning to Paris. Instead, he stopped practicing architecture—in favor of art—that same year.

His work has been exhibited in Paris salon showings, and in galleries in Houston, New York, Chicago, and Boston. His work also has been shown in group exhibitions at the De Cordova Museum and Currier Gallery of Art.

◀ **Ben Freeman**
Unfinished Works: Lanette
36" x 36" (91 cm x 91 cm)

Karen McCarthy
141 Warren Street
Arlington, MA 02174

A Boston-area native, Karen McCarthy attended the Massachusetts College of Art, Boston, and the Haystack Mountain School of Crafts in Deer Isle, Maine. McCarthy exhibits her work in galleries and non-profit exhibition spaces throughout the United States; her art is well represented in both private and public collections.

◀ **Karen McCarthy**
Solitaire: For Lenore Tawney
Paper with pigmented starch paste, thread, and colored pencil
26" x 26" (66 cm x 66 cm)

Rachel Paxton
4 Harris Avenue
Jamaica Plain, MA 02130
617-427-1065
or:
c/o Clark Gallery
P. O. Box 339
145 Lincoln Road
Lincoln, MA 01773
617-259-8303

Born and raised in Greenwich, Connecticut, Rachel Paxton studied textile design at the Rhode Island School of Design, Providence, Rhode Island. She later attended the School of the Museum of Fine Arts, Boston. Although she uses only paper in her collages, her fabric design background is evident in her work. She has exhibited her work widely in galleries and museums through the United States.

Rachel Paxton ▶
Split Middle Ground, 2:00
Paper with mixed media
43" x 29" (109 cm x 74 cm)

138

Deborah Putnoi
171 Fayerweather Street
Cambridge, MA 02138-1242
617-876-2006
or:
c/o Clark Gallery
P. O. Box 339
145 Lincoln Road
Lincoln, MA 01773

Deborah Putnoi attended Tufts University, Medford, Massachusetts, and the School of the Museum of Fine Arts, Boston, where she earned a BA in Political Science and BFA in Studio Art. She then attended the SMFA where she obtained her fifth year diploma in painting and printmaking. In 1990, Putnoi earned a Master of Education degree from the Harvard Graduate School of Education. She worked for a number of years at Harvard Project Zero where she did research on community art centers in economically disadvantaged communities and on museum education.

▼ **Deborah Putnoi**
green t and black j
Monoprint
11" x 15" (28 cm x 38 cm)

Clara Wainwright
57 Upland Road
Brookline, MA 02146
617-628-0060

Clara Wainwright is an artist with a strong commitment to community involvement, and has created community quilt projects with both adults and teenagers. She began working in fabric collage with little formal training. Born and raised in Boston, Wainwright studied literature at the University of North Carolina, and did not become interested in quilting until she was given a quilt when her son was born. She has created pillows, books, and community and youth quilts that have been exhibited in museums and university galleries throughout the Northeast.

Clara Wainwright ▶
Entrance to a Folly Cove Garden
Fabric collage
31" x 31" (79 cm x 79 cm)

◎ EXPLORING ◎ CREATIVITY

THERE ARE A FEW THINGS ABOUT COLLAGE that are unique to it as an expressive medium. One of the most obvious—and gratifying to many—is that you don't have to be able to draw to make a good collage. (In fact, one of the most famous collage artists, Joseph Cornell, never learned to draw.) This isn't to say that many collage artists aren't also excellent draftspeople; a number of the artists in this book combine their work with painting and drawing to beautiful effect. But if you're self-conscious about your drawing skills—or maybe you don't have room in your house for a studio setup—it's great to know that there's a way to make art that can be as simple as tearing up an old magazine and pasting together the images to say something new.

Artistry in collage can have multiple moments of inspiration. One of these has to do with creative collecting. Quite different from collecting baseball cards or McCoy vases, creative collecting is the searching out of interesting objects for possible use in making art. "Broken Melody" (page 145) by Judi Riesch is a perfect example of what can result when a collector has an eye for the latent magic of castoffs. The focal point of her assembled piece is a vintage photo album she unearthed at a flea market. What made the album remarkable to Riesch is that it contained a music box inside its cover, so she exposed the guts and embellished them with strung wire and wax drippings to draw attention to their distinctiveness. Though as an album the item had outlived its usefulness, Riesch recognized the beauty inherent in the object and created an artwork around it, giving it new meaning and worth.

What Riesch experienced when she saw the album's potential is a moment of recognition that is another example of the creative inspiration fundamental to collage making. Whether wandering through a flea market or just sifting through boxes of collected ephemera while working, the artist will suddenly see an item as right—the right shape, the right statement, the right fit. Deborah Putnoi's work depends on her ability to make these recognitions. For "Enmeshed" (page 154), she let the materials inspire her, using items as diverse as pieces of embroidery, etched metal plates, and torn up drawings made specifically to use as collage elements. Working within a grid structure, she moved around the various elements and layered some sections with paint until she found a composition that worked. Her process is an intuitive one, developed over years of working as an artist. Open-ended meanings, multiple statements, and surprising combinations are all part of the creative mix in her work that makes it so evocative.

When a collage is finished, a transformation has occurred: Where there once was a random collection of found or created objects and images, there is now a cohesive whole. This creation is something more than the sum of its disparate parts and is able to express a theme or meaning that none of its components conveys alone. Chantale Légaré's "Crossings" (page 151) is a house-shaped structure, colorfully painted, embellished with beads and etching, and filled with evocative imagery. With its *mendhi*-painted foot, map fragments, and diverse found objects, the box delights in all things connected to travel and discovery. But as a whole, it is a shrine to the creative process. Through use of a vivid palette, close attention to detail, and a keen appreciation of her materials, Légaré celebrates the creative journey that takes the artist to known and unknown places, wherever they may be.

As you express your own creativity, something to consider is the way in which images resonate for you. If you find yourself repeatedly drawn to certain objects and images, these might be the beginnings of a personal vocabulary. Even working with already established systems of symbols can be a useful tool in sparking ideas. For "Silent Book" (page 142), Paula Grasdal relied on images gleaned from alchemy. Though this is imagery anyone has access to, filtering it through her own particular artistic sensibility allowed her to create a personal vision that can

still be decoded by anyone with a knowledge of alchemy. Furthermore, there's something essential about the images that translates, even when the "real" meaning is missed. A viewer might not understand that the "crown of perfection" has alchemical significance, but certainly there are cultural associations with crowns that have to do with royalty, leadership, and honor. Along with any other meanings, the outspread golden wings evoke a sense of freedom and flight.

Whatever your status as artist—whether you are just starting out or are a seasoned pro—collage is a medium that will stimulate your imagination and help you to expand your artistic vision. Its reliance on creative juxtapositions of objects and images, combined with how easily it includes the creative tools from other mediums, gives it a versatility that offers the maker a wide range of creative expression. As you integrate items, objects, or images into the collage, the artistic choices you make are a function of the creative soul at work.

✺ SILENT BOOK ✺

This altered book collage was made using
textured tiles prepared by pressing found objects
onto paper covered in modeling paste. To create
a system of symbols, Paula Grasdal adapted
images taken from alchemy, the medieval pursuit
of the transmutation of base metals into gold
and the transformation of the spiritual self.
The gold-leafed heraldic crown or "crown of
perfection" represents the unification of opposites
while the wings allude to the upward flight of the
spirit and the process of elements transforming in
the alchemical vessel. The diptych format and
contrasting colors emphasize the duality in
alchemy and the coming together of opposites.

Dimensions: 9 ½" × 13" (24 cm × 33 cm) | Artist: Paula Grasdal

STEPS	MATERIALS

STEPS

1. Using PVA, cover the inside of an old book with the wrinkled paper. Coat the inside and outside of the book with gesso, let dry, and then paint as desired with acrylics.

2. Cut rag paper into several small strips and two larger pieces. Spread a thin layer of modeling paste on some of the papers with a palette knife, and then press textured objects such as leaves, stencils, fabric, art stamps or screening into the wet paste. Spread acrylic medium on the remaining strips, creating textures with the palette knife. When the papers are dry, paint them with washes of acrylic paints and highlight the textures by dry-brushing gesso or rubbing oil pastels on the raised areas.

3. Crease and then rip the prepared strips into squares. Using fabric glue, collage them to the inside of the book, making sure to balance colors and textures on each side. To create a diptych effect, leave the inside spine uncovered. Cut out arch shapes (or other framing shapes) from the larger textured papers and glue in place.

4. Decide on a system of symbols—any theme will work with this project so the possible approaches are limitless. Draw motifs on rag paper and cut out. Apply gold-leaf sizing to the cutout shapes, selected areas of the collage, and the inside of the spine. When the sizing is tacky, apply the imitation gold leaf, removing excess leaf with a soft artist's brush. After the sizing has set, lightly burnish the gold leaf with a cotton ball. Attach the gold motifs to the collage with fabric glue. Block-print a design with brown and gold acrylics down the length of the spine.

VARIATIONS

Instead of small pieces of paper, try texturing two larger sheets with the modeling paste or substitute found objects for the cutout paper motifs.

MATERIALS

- ☺ old book cover
- ☺ rag paper (such as watercolor or printmaking papers)
- ☺ medium-weight wrinkled paper
- ☺ motifs of your choice
- ☺ modeling paste
- ☺ gesso
- ☺ acrylic paints
- ☺ oil pastels
- ☺ imitation gold leaf
- ☺ palette knife
- ☺ carved eraser (for block-printed design)
- ☺ adhesives: acrylic gel medium, fabric glue (such as Sobo), diluted PVA, leaf sizing
- ☺ basic collage supplies (see page 12)

❧❧ BROKEN MELODY ❧❧

Like many collage artists, Judi Riesch often finds inspiration in a single object. Here, it was the discarded back of a vintage music-box photo album she discovered at a flea market. She found its mechanical inner workings unusual and beautiful, and decided to create a loose narrative inside the album using an old photograph, antique textile fragments, and words and numbers cut from vintage papers. To house the album, she created an intimate interior space by collaging a shadow box frame with vintage ledger pages and sheet music. A decorative gold frame lends the piece a Victorian feel, yet her use of wire embellishments and beeswax drippings is distinctively modern.

Dimensions: 18" h × 15" w × 2" d (46 cm × 38 cm × 5 cm)　|　Artist: Judi Riesch

STEPS	MATERIALS
1. Start by finding or making something special to use as the heart of your assemblage. Expose the guts of an old clock or telephone or take several interesting old items and join them together. Once you have your center, find or make a shadow box frame.	◎ found object or objects for center of assemblage ◎ shadow box frame ◎ heavy mat board ◎ assorted vintage ribbons and trims ◎ vintage papers
2. Cut a piece of heavy mat board to fit in the shadow box. Collage vintage papers onto the mat board using acrylic medium and cover the insides of the frame as well. Add details or washes of color, as desired, with colored pencils and acrylic paints.	◎ acrylic paints ◎ colored pencils ◎ beeswax ◎ stencils ◎ wire

3. Wire or glue the back of your centerpiece to the board. Build up the assemblage by adhering found objects, ribbons, and trim around the centerpiece (and within its workings if appropriate). Take as much time as you need—hours or even days—to move and reposition objects before adhering them. Finding the perfect arrangement is a combination of association, color, texture, and discovery.

4. To draw attention to what's being contained within, the artist stuck upholstery tacks along two sides of the opening in the album and strung wire across it. Another detail: She applied melted beeswax to the area around the opening with a small brush, which she then incised with a sharp point and rubbed with acrylic paint. Experiment freely with your materials to add textures and color until the piece feels complete.

5. Once you are satisfied, fit the entire base into the shadow box frame. Attach a wire or a saw-tooth hanger for hanging.

MATERIALS (continued)

◎ brass upholstery tacks
◎ adhesives: acrylic gel medium, glue, adhesive caulk
◎ basic collage supplies (see page 12)

◎ Judi Riesch's Creativity Tips

As a collector and keeper of fragments from the past, I find myself using these objects as a continuing source of ideas and inspiration. When creativity is challenged, I have only to look at the things I love. Something will spark an idea, a memory, often surprising me as it unfolds and takes on a new life. My involvement with this music box stemmed from a memory of one my grandmother gave me when I was a child—a tiny ballerina twirling inside a glass dome to the "Vienna Life Waltz."

ඹඥ TEMPLE ඥඹ

*To get the right materials for this paper-pulp
collage, which emulates the look of an ancient
relic or temple, Paula Grasdal made them
herself. She created a set of cast handmade
papers and used diversely textured objects to add
relief textures to the wet paper pulp. Once the
papers were dry, she transformed them with
acrylic paints and oil pastels, arranged them in a
composition, and then glued them together.
Though working with fragile, almost transitory
materials, Grasdal has established a sense of
timelessness by emphasizing the tactile nature of
the materials and using a palette that evokes
earth, sky, and water.*

Dimensions: 13" × 12" (33 cm × 30 cm) | Artist: Paula Grasdal

TEMPLE ☺

STEPS

1. Tear the cotton linters into stamp-size pieces and soak in water for at least three hours. Place a handful of soaked linters in a blender full of water, blend until smooth, and pour the contents into a basin of tepid water. Repeat with the remaining linters, adding more water to the basin as needed. When finished, add methyl cellulose to strengthen pulp for casting.

2. Stir the pulp and water mixture, and then slide the stretched metal mesh into the basin, scooping up pulp as you lift it out. Shake the mesh gently to even out the coating of pulp on its surface. Flip the wet pulp onto a piece of felt, pressing a sponge onto the back of the mesh to help release it.

3. To cast the paper, carefully flip the damp pulp sheet off its felt backing onto a textured surface and gently press the paper into the recessed areas. Reinforce the pulp with another sheet of damp pulp if necessary. Repeat with various textured surfaces until you have at least ten embossed sheets (you can also add botanical elements such as petals, herbs, and leaves to the pulp for a beautiful effect). Leave to dry; this can take about three days but will go faster if the sheets are placed near a heat source or out in the sun.

4. When the papers are dry, gently pry them loose from the textured objects. Paint with acrylic paints, and then highlight raised areas with metallic paints or oil pastels.

5. Arrange the painted papers together to create a temple or other shape and adhere with PVA glue.

TIPS

To create handmade paper forms, cut the metal mesh into shapes (such as an arch) and use without a frame to scoop up the pulp. As an alternative to painting the dry papers, you can color the pulp in the basin with paper dyes, but you will need to use several separate basins for this method.

MATERIALS

- ☺ three sheets of cotton linters for making pulp
- ☺ papermaking felts or disposable dishcloths
- ☺ sponges
- ☺ metal screen stretched in a frame or cut into an arch shape
- ☺ methyl cellulose
- ☺ acrylic and metallic paints
- ☺ oil pastels
- ☺ objects with textured surfaces for casting (the artist used carved wood blocks, burlap fabric, and embossed tin)
- ☺ square basin
- ☺ blender
- ☺ adhesive: PVA glue
- ☺ basic collage supplies (see page 12)

⟨⟨ CROSSINGS ⟩⟩

*Chantale Légaré's multi–media assemblage
combines painted images with map fragments
and found objects to comment on how the places
we grow up in or travel to can shape who we are
and how we think. The house shape represents a
starting point or home, a place in which living,
dreaming, and remembering can occur. Légaré
uses a paint palette of vibrant colors reminiscent
of Indian textiles, a notion that's reinforced by
the image of a foot covered with* mendhi
*patterns. Roads and rivers cut from maps lead
away from the painted foot, symbolizing the
many pathways walked.*

Dimensions: 13 ¼" h × 10" w × 3" d (33½ cm × 25 cm × 8 cm) | Artist: Chantale Légaré

STEPS

1. Build or find a small wooden house that opens from the back. Cut a piece of glass to fit inside the front; add frosted designs using glass-etching solution, contact paper cut into stencils, and a brush. Rinse the glass thoroughly and set aside. Sand and paint the house as desired. Affix the glass inside the front with a small narrow molding just like a frame.

2. Cut a piece of lauan to fit inside the box. Add collage elements that say something about the place you are commemorating. The artist used painted architectural moldings, brass bells, and a rectangle painting she made of a small foot decorated with Indian *mendhi* patterns over fragments cut from maps of places important to her. (When she travels, the artist collects materials and artifacts to use in her work.)

3. To decorate with beads, drill holes along the box's sides. String glass beads on fishing line and attach them through the holes.

4. Seal the final collage inside the house with brackets and another piece of lauan placed behind the work. Attach an eyehook and wire for hanging.

TIPS

If another idea occurs to you while working and it's too late to make a change, write it down and save it for another piece. If you find you are "painting" too much, cut out holes to make small windows of tranquility in the work. You can use those cutouts later in other projects.

MATERIALS

- ☺ 3³⁄₄" × 48" (9½ cm × 122 cm) birch plywood, ½" (1 cm) thick
- ☺ two pieces 12" × 7¼" (30 cm × 18½ cm) lauan
- ☺ wood molding
- ☺ glass, glasscutter, and gloves
- ☺ glass-etching solution and contact paper
- ☺ acrylic paints in various colors
- ☺ embellishments such as brass bells, bits of maps, glass beads
- ☺ fishing line
- ☺ screws and nails
- ☺ brackets
- ☺ eyehook and wire
- ☺ handsaw
- ☺ miter saw
- ☺ handheld drill
- ☺ nail gun or hammer
- ☺ adhesives: acrylic gel medium, wood glue
- ☺ basic collage supplies (see page 12)

☺ Chantale Légaré's Creativity Tips

I look at my travel photo albums, art journals filled with my ideas, and old work. I always keep notes of things to do or make when I have time. I look at great masterpieces and try to figure out why they still work. At the library, I read *National Geographic* magazine to learn about other peoples and customs, textiles, and patterns. When I have a creative block, I go for a walk or work in the garden, where my hands can be creative while my mind is finding some peace.

ɔ☉ ENMESHED ☉ɔ

Deborah Putnoi created this colorful collaged box using a grid pattern as her organizing principle. She collected images (often her own work that she tears up to use as collage fragments), texts, fabric swatches, monoprints, and etched metal plates, then adhered them randomly, reflecting the randomness of life and creating a kind of sensory bombardment. In her work, disparate fragments and seemingly unrelated images— a sketched sheep, a painted portrait, the letter W—coexist within the loose grid much as multiple events coexist within a single moment in time. Putnoi believes her work is not complete until there is a viewer: someone who takes the assembled elements and constructs their own meaning based on personal associations and history.

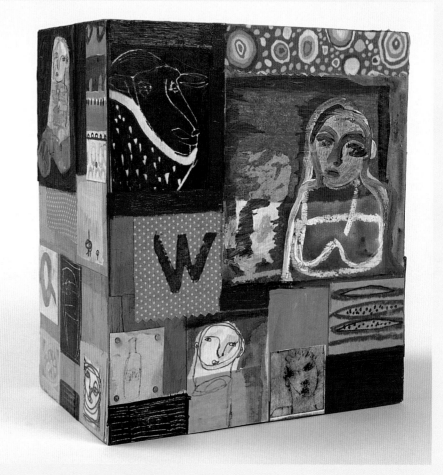

Dimensions: 9" h × 8" w × 5" d (23 cm × 20 cm × 13 cm) | Artist: Deborah Putnoi

ENMESHED ☺

STEPS

1. Gesso a wooden box, etching images into the wet gesso with a stylus. Let dry.

2. While the gesso dries, use various sized brushes and rollers to paint assorted papers that you will cut up and use in the collage. (See the Creativity Tips box for more ideas for making collage materials.)

3. Push acrylic paint or oil sticks into the incised dry gesso and wipe away excess.

4. Gather collage materials such as painted papers, old drawings, fabric, phone book pages, cardboard, old prints, etc. Start arranging the elements on the front of the box. This piece uses a basic grid format, which allows for free expression within a simple structure. Work with the grid, or experiment with other forms. Don't plan things too much and work intuitively. Take chances—you can always paint over what doesn't work. Use acrylic medium to adhere the collage materials to the box. (Tip: Acrylic medium comes in gloss or matte finish; experiment with both and use what works best for your piece.)

5. Paint the spaces around the collage elements to add another dimension. Finish by painting and collaging the sides and top of the box.

MATERIALS

- ☺ wooden box
- ☺ old drawings, prints, texts from books or journals, handpainted collage papers
- ☺ fabric
- ☺ gesso
- ☺ acrylic paint
- ☺ oil sticks
- ☺ stylus
- ☺ adhesive: acrylic gel medium
- ☺ basic collage supplies (see page 12)

☺ Deborah Putnoi's Creativity Tips

Do twenty one-minute drawings of your face, then rip up the pieces when you're done and create a collage from these elements. Do two-handed drawings: Draw whatever comes into your head using both hands concurrently. Let your hands keep moving. Do this exercise a few times and watch what develops. Put music on, get some tempera paint, thick brushes, and newsprint. Close your eyes and paint to the music. When the paintings are dry, rip them up and use them as collage materials.

THE CREATIVE PROCESS

DEBORAH PUTNOI

Ripping a drawing in half, a corner catches my eye, a finely drawn face of a boy next to a splash of red paint. I find an old monoprint and cut a square from it. I place the torn and cut fragments on a wooden surface, rearranging them until a composition reveals itself. I grab an old aluminum plate with an etching of a hand on it, nail it onto the surface, and glue a section of black fabric next to it. Then I take my brush, fill it with a wad of gesso, and paint the wood. Into this wet layer, I etch a drawing of a cell dividing in mitosis. Once it's dry, I rub paint into the grooves of the drawing, adding another texture. I am intrigued by the juxtaposition not only of random images but also of a multiplicity of textures and materials. My world is ripe with an abundance of images, elements, ideas, and materials—and my work attempts to capture this infinite array.

Where does the creative impulse come from? My brain, my soul, my hands embedded in the materials, the motion of making something? For me, the act of creation is a letting go. Jumping into "the unknown," I hold my breath hoping that something powerful will form out of the chatter in my mind. As I navigate my way, fragments of paper and fabric, tin and canvas surround my workspace until finally, in the mess, I discover the clarity that is the final composition.

My creative process is powered by the ability to take chances and allow randomness to exist within a formal grid structure. Usually, I work on many art pieces at one time, moving fragments from one to the next until I sense that an element works in a specific piece. I never sketch things out ahead of time and I thrive on seeing what unfolds spontaneously. I will draw a variety of images on different types of paper (phone books, tracing paper, graph paper). I will also experiment with a wide range of materials (oil stick, watercolor, tempera paint, silkscreen, potato prints) on larger pieces of paper, making abstract pieces I know I will cut up and use as fragments later. In my studio, I have a giant drawer that houses old drawings, monoprints, silkscreens, works on paper, sketches, fabric, and etching plates. As I work, I sift through my old discards and remember creating each one. Reusing them allows me to witness the regeneration of different themes and ideas in my work over time.

When I think critically about my process, I realize there are some core elements that fuel my creativity: courage, discipline, and passion. Creating something takes courage and confidence. Taking that leap into the unknown each time we create something new is a courageous act. When I go to the studio, I try to start working before I can think about it, because once my mind gets too involved I start to question and control every move I make. It's like plunging into the lake at the beginning of summer. If I slowly inch my way in and feel the water a little bit at a time, I may decide that it's too cold and I won't go in at all. But when I just jump in, I realize that the experience is exhilarating and the water feels great.

One reason people often hold back is a fear of making mistakes. But the idea of "mistakes" is almost not valid: A mistake is an unforeseen opportunity. It is a way to generate previously unimagined ideas and to find and create new possibilities. Sometimes I will draw with my left hand to purposely make mistakes or to make my drawing more eccentric. I search out the uninvited marks or disturbing color to see how that will add an element of surprise to the composition. As Shaun McNiff says in his book *Trust the Process: An Artist's Guide to Letting Go*, "In the creative process, one action leads to another, and the final outcome is shaped by a chain of expressions that could never be planned in advance." Openness to mistakes, mess, chaos, and the unknown all allow the process to flow and unfold.

At the same time, discipline is essential. Having an idea that you would like to make something is only the first step. Getting in there and doing it, and continuing to do it, is almost the most important aspect of creativity. It's about going to the "office"—be it the studio, the cafe, the outdoors—and working. For me, at times, this is the hardest part of being an artist. It is difficult to face work that is not progressing and there are times I just don't "feel" creative. But the discipline of holding to a set studio time, of going there and making something (anything), is important in keeping the creative process dynamic.

Finally, involvement in the creative process requires passion for the whole endeavor. I need to rip paper and collage the torn shreds onto a white canvas. I need to feel the paint sliding over the textured surface, to thrust my brush into the heart of the composition. I crave the feeling of my materials. I love to mix colors and watch the subtle ways they can change by just the slightest addition or subtraction of another color. I had a teacher at art school who said to a fellow student, "If it is a choice to paint, then don't choose it. Painting chooses you—it is an inexplicable need."

For each person the creative process is a unique exploration. Each of us has an individual fingerprint and the way we work in expressing ourselves is also singular. As I place the final element into the composition, I step back and look at the piece as a whole. I start to make connections among the shapes and forms, and in my mind's eye I glimpse another way the work could be resolved. I grab another canvas, pick up an old drawing and cut out a section, collage it onto the surface, and I am off creating the next piece—one in a chain of pieces that I make as an outgrowth of the creative process, which is central to my existence.

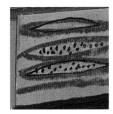

⦿ CHRONICLING ⦿ RELATIONSHIPS

T HE CONNECTIONS BETWEEN and among people, and between people and the world they live in, are the subject of the following chapter. With these projects, the artists seek to honor special relationships in their lives and to divine the meaning of connectedness and relating. Projects range from personal portraits of a specific loved one to overviews of how identity is affected by the societal rules and expectations that shape human relations.

Although the personal nature of some of these works makes them seemingly less accessible to the viewer, who likely will not know particular details, their atmosphere of intimacy serves to draw the viewer in, allowing a more intuitive understanding to occur. In "The Chess Lesson" (page 166), Paula Grasdal put together an affectionate portrait of her father that reflects his love of his profession—teaching math and physics—and of chess. Because we know the game requires two players, the presence of the artist is implied as that second player, the recipient of the lesson. Encountering the board head on, the viewer experiences the piece from the artist's perspective, that is, "across the chess board" from the father. And even though the youthful man looking back at us is a stranger, we experience him in the role of father by bringing our own memories and feelings about our fathers to the piece. In this way, a particularly private vision becomes universally accessible.

While some artists choose a subtly implied presence (or aren't present at all) in their collages, many others successfully place themselves inside a piece, granting further insight into the story of a relationship by spelling out their place within it. Maria G. Keehan uses a photograph of herself looking up at representations of memories and stories about her grandmothers, in "What I Think I Know About Elizabeth and Maggie" (page 169), to show how she is seeking to know them and how half of her comes from each of them. Meredith Hamilton ("Le Mariage," page 172) uses an image of herself as a princess bride (a playful nod to notions of fairytale romance) on top of a wedding cake carousel, which represents relationships as filtered through the lens of marriage. Her knight wears shining armor with a twist: He sports a literal "blockhead."

Taking on the theme of a relationship to a place rather than a person, Grasdal's "Pond Life" (page 160) honors an island along the Pacific Northwest Coast where she spent time as a child. Nestling a portrait of lily pads among repeated images of the pond's lush surface and encasing the whole in layers of colorful encaustic paints, the artist built an abstraction of water and plant life that evokes rather than re-creates the actual pond. The only visitor is a dragonfly, hovering in place over the blue water. A symbol of regeneration and change, the dragonfly represents the biological cycles in the real pond and also changes to the pond as it exists in the memory of the artist.

Objects and images within an assemblage or collage can carry meanings according to where they are positioned in a piece. Hamilton's wedding cake collage uses the tiers of the cake to establish a social structure wherein the married couple is the center, their children are the second tier, and friends, career, financial decisions, and home make up the final group of forces at play in the couple's life. Another artist's collage of the same subject could look very different if, for example, there were no children and so career or friends played a larger role. In Keehan's piece, the placement of images and objects hints at discrete narratives within the whole: At the center of each half is the grandmother whose life is featured; the background is their actual "background" (photos of their birthplace); and surrounding details tell of journeys (a ship at sea, a map of destinations, parts of a diary) and religious faith (a rosary, an image of the Virgin Mary).

The choices you make about how to approach your subject will greatly affect the outcome, so take time when you're getting started to think about what you want to say. When working on a place collage, think about what aspects of the place are most meaningful to you. Consider various times of day and photographs taken under different weather conditions. What mood do they establish? Which ones best represent how you feel about the place?

If people are a part of the appeal, include them. Grasdal focused on a pond in her place collage, but Bowen Island also has beautiful forests and beaches she could have highlighted for dramatically different results. A series of three or four collages could show the island's varied topography and offers an interesting alternative approach.

When chronicling a relationship with a person, consider it from a variety of angles: Do you want to portray a relationship as it is (or was) or an idealized vision of what you wish for it? What details and images will offer insight into the personalities of the people in your collage? And where are you—a part of the story or, like the viewer, outside of it? The key is to follow your instincts, letting the collage develop with each new addition or change. And nothing says you have to focus outward: A relationship collage can also offer a way to examine aspects of your own personality and life, allowing you to explore your relationship to yourself. Whatever your approach, as you are positioning images, textures, and objects in layer after layer, you'll find yourself engaged in an intuitive process that may begin with a specific idea but will undoubtedly lead to a discovery of much more.

❧❧ POND LIFE ❧❧

This lushly hued piece, encaustic and collage on plywood, celebrates the artist's relationship to a special place—Bowen Island, located on the Pacific Northwest Coast. Recalling childhood explorations of the island's natural wonders, Paula Grasdal focused on images of a pond, carpeted with lily pads and whirring with iridescent dragonflies. The combined elements of photocopied photographs, incised drawing, and translucent wax create a tactile layered effect characteristic of the encaustic technique.

The repeated lily pad image and the translucent blues and greens of the encaustic paints lend the piece tranquility, evoking thoughts of quiet contemplation and feeling connected to the natural world.

Dimensions: 13" × 10¾" (33 cm × 27½ cm) | Artist: Paula Grasdal

STEPS

1. To begin this project, read about encaustic technique on page 175. Make multiple photocopies of various photographs of a place that is meaningful to you. Enlarge or shrink them to vary the composition. To create the background design, arrange the photocopies in a repeat pattern on plywood and trim them to fit. Glue the background papers in place with PVA, roll with a brayer, and let dry. Reserve the main image for use in Step 3.

2. Paint a layer of hot encaustic medium over the collaged papers and the board's edges. Blend pre-mixed encaustic colors with encaustic medium for a translucent effect, and paint the tinted wax onto the first wax layer. Fuse the layers together with a heat gun.

3. Apply the main image by heating a section of the wax background with a heat gun and pressing the paper onto this heated area. Encapsulate the paper by painting hot wax medium over its surface. Fuse with a heat gun.

4. Cut out selected shapes from your photocopies (the artist chose lily pads) and collage these on top of the main image and elsewhere on the composition, using the same method as in Step 3. You can also use pressed leaves, old letters, maps, etc. Engrave an image with a stylus into the wax (such as the dragonfly) and rub an oil pastel over the incised lines. Wipe away the excess pastel with a linseed-oil-soaked cloth.

5. Create a border by painting opaque wax in a contrasting color around the board's edges and sides. Fuse with a heat gun and let cool. To create a surface sheen, polish the wax with a soft cloth.

TIPS

Wax is not compatible with acrylics (including acrylic gesso) but can be combined or layered with oil paints and oil sticks. To clean your brushes, dip them in a tin of hot paraffin and wipe the bristles with paper towels.

MATERIALS

- ☺ black-and-white or color photocopies of photographs
- ☺ piece of ³⁄₄" (2 cm) plywood for backing
- ☺ oil pastels
- ☺ linseed oil
- ☺ encaustic paints and medium
- ☺ heated palette (for heating wax)
- ☺ heat gun with variable speeds
- ☺ natural bristle brushes
- ☺ stylus
- ☺ adhesive: PVA glue
- ☺ basic collage supplies (see page 12)

❧ 4 DRESSES ❧

Dresses are metaphorically laden with meaning about feminine identity, from issues related to physical appearance to expectations about women's roles and relationships. To suggest how societal forces shape women from childhood onward, Jane Maxwell uses a repeated paper doll–dress form as her central image. She manipulates the images with colorful vellums and photocopied imagery, then layers them over various found papers such as texts, sewing patterns, and printed images. Despite the rigorousness of the dress form and its insistence on conformity, individual "personalities" are visible through the vellum and successfully subvert the form.

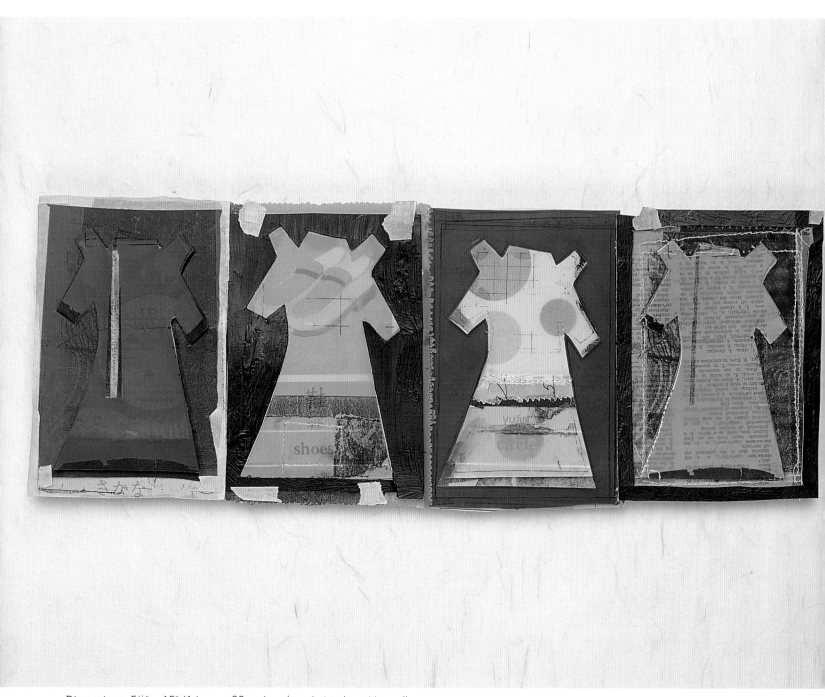

Dimensions: 5½" × 15" (14 cm × 38 cm) | Artist: Jane Maxwell

4 DRESSES ⑨

STEPS

1. Select imagery from a variety of sources—magazines, books, found papers. Seek out imagery that relates to an overall message, for example, "4 Dresses" features writing from sewing patterns and related circle imagery, representing the whole person beneath the cutout form.

2. Photocopy chosen images onto vellum in various colors. Play around with varying image size, using color and black-and-white copies, and combining or layering images right on the copy machine. Another good layering material is clear acetate, which photocopies well and offers a slick contrasting texture.

3. Find a central image to repeat (in this case, an actual doll-dress form) or create your own. Choose something that speaks to you—a tree, a window, a tiara. Repeated imagery will have impact in a line of two, three, or four, and also two over two.

4. Build repeating forms by layering found papers under and over the central image and by utilizing negative spaces. Create dimension and contrast with acrylic paint or charcoal.

5. Join the repeated images using a variety of binding materials (tape, stitching, glue). Be creative: Household items such as straight pins, masking tape, and staples add texture and interest.

MATERIALS

- ⑨ vellum, clear and assorted colors
- ⑨ background imagery from books, postcards, sewing patterns
- ⑨ photocopies of various images
- ⑨ acrylic paints
- ⑨ charcoal pencil
- ⑨ thread and sewing machine
- ⑨ adhesive: PVA glue
- ⑨ basic collage supplies (see page 12)

⑨ Jane Maxwell's Creativity Tips

Don't limit yourself to solid colored papers: Transparent vellum and acetate papers are also available in a variety of patterns and become high-impact layering pieces when transformed by a photocopied image. Another tip: Take a pre-existing piece of your art, place it on a copy machine, and transfer it onto a variety of papers. It's a great starting point for future pieces. And keep your eyes open for unique paper and images. Flea markets and antiques malls are great for digging up vintage signs, posters, books, ledgers, etc. Old papers have a special color and textural quality that adds depth, richness, and history to a collage.

✪ THE CHESS LESSON ✪

This richly colored fabric collage pays homage to the artist's father, a physics and math teacher and an avid chess player. Paula Grasdal used photo transfer techniques to create the portrait of her father as a young man and the silhouettes of chess pieces. Transferred images of physics equations evoke a classroom blackboard and together with pieces of metallic mesh build a containing border for the chessboard. The board's grid pattern organizes the disparate elements of the piece and also reflects her father's logical and thoughtful approach to life.

Dimensions: 12" × 12" (30 cm × 30 cm) | Artist: Paula Grasdal

THE CHESS LESSON ☺

STEPS

1. To transfer a photocopy of a portrait, brush a small piece of canvas and the photocopy with acrylic matte medium, and place the image face down on the coated fabric. Press out air bubbles and let dry thoroughly (about 24 hours). Soak the canvas in warm water and gently rub off the paper until the image is exposed (it will be reversed). Let dry, then tint the portrait with diluted acrylic paints.

2. Cut white silk organza pieces and other collage elements for the border. Transfer desired images using the technique described on page 215. Tint the organza with diluted silk paints, let dry, and set with an iron.

3. Choose a base pattern or design that says something about the person or relationship in your collage. To make a chessboard pattern, draw a grid on a 12" × 12" (30 cm × 30 cm) piece of canvas, leaving a 2" (5 cm) border. Paint the checkerboard pattern and border with acrylics in colors of your choice. When dry, iron the fabric on the unpainted side to flatten.

4. Make or buy a stencil for the border design and stencil the design using metallic acrylic paint. Let dry.

5. Brush fabric glue onto the canvas border and adhere the organza photo transfers made in Step 2. Apply other decorative fabrics where desired. Embellish the portrait (the artist used fragments of a photocopy on acetate and some metallic organza) and adhere it to the composition. As a finishing touch, glue on found metal objects using the industrial-strength glue.

VARIATIONS

Add hand or machine embroidery as another layer of embellishment. Areas of fabric can also be stitched and then cut away to reveal contrasting fabrics underneath (this is called reverse-appliqué; see "Relic IV" on page 250).

MATERIALS

- ☺ canvas
- ☺ silk organza or other natural fiber cloth, in white and metallic gold
- ☺ fiberglass mesh
- ☺ found objects for embellishments
- ☺ photocopies of photographs and other design elements
- ☺ images (such as chess pieces) photo-copied on clear acetate
- ☺ decorative stencil for border design
- ☺ stencil brush
- ☺ acrylic paints
- ☺ fabric or silk paints
- ☺ acrylic matte medium and oil of wintergreen (for transferring images)
- ☺ burnishing tool
- ☺ adhesives: fabric glue, industrial-strength craft glue
- ☺ basic collage supplies (see page 12)

⊚⊚ WHAT I THINK I KNOW ⊚⊚ ABOUT ELIZABETH AND MAGGIE

Maria G. Keehan set out to make this multi-media collage about her grandmothers by limiting herself solely to what she remembered from family lore rather than validating those memories by making inquiries. Using a silverware case as her container, she dedicated one side to each grandmother and filled it with ephemera that recalled stories or images she associated with each: a rosary, pieces of china, and a portrait of Rudolph Valentino for Elizabeth; some old buttons, scraps from a travel diary, and photos of the coal mining town where she grew up for Maggie. With dreamlike imagery, multiple layers, and colorful found objects, Keehan evokes an intimate vision of her family heritage.

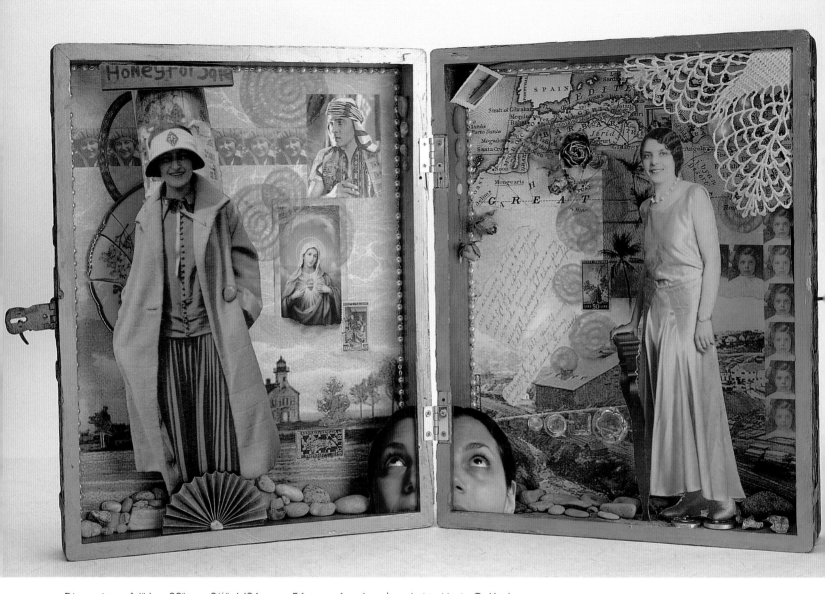

Dimensions: 14" h × 22" w × 2½" d (36 cm × 56 cm × 6 cm) | Artist: Maria G. Keehan

WHAT I THINK I KNOW ABOUT ELIZABETH AND MAGGIE ☺

STEPS

1. Find a suitable container: an old silverware case, wooden cigar box, painted metal tin. Clean up the insides and paint with gold-leaf paint. Cover hot-press illustration board with marbleized or other paper and glue it into the back of your box.

2. Assemble photographs and found images. Choose a portrait and have an iris print or color photocopy made to size. Using acrylic medium, mount it on Bristol board backed with gold tissue paper. Cut out with a craft knife.

3. If you can, use a computer to alter photographs in creative ways. The artist downloaded images to Photoshop, played with them, and embellished printouts with colored pencils. She also colorized black-and-white images (of Rudolph Valentino) and created strips of small headshots of her grandmothers. Many of these effects can be reproduced manually with the help of a color photocopier.

4. Do research to find out things, such as what the town where your person was born was like and other historical facts that relate to their life, or rely on your memories alone. Copy passages from their favorite book. If possible, obtain photocopies from diaries or letters in their handwriting.

5. Assemble all of your materials (including relevant found objects) and play with arrangements in the box. Glue things down slowly, considering the composition as you work. Let pieces relate to each other to create a narrative about the person or relationship you're commemorating. Draw attention to details through interesting placement (such  as the ship in the corner seen here), juxtaposition, and repetition.

MATERIALS

- ☺ case to house collage
- ☺ color printouts or photocopies of photographs and diary entries
- ☺ iris prints (high-end digital prints; color photocopies may be substituted)
- ☺ found objects and embellishments such as buttons, stamps, stones, rosary beads, old photographs
- ☺ decorative papers such as embossed tissue paper, gold tissue paper, marbleized paper
- ☺ gold-leaf paint
- ☺ colored pencil
- ☺ Bristol board and hot-press illustration board
- ☺ heavyweight rag paper
- ☺ sandpaper
- ☺ brass hinges
- ☺ friend with digital camera
- ☺ adhesives: acrylic matte medium, craft glue, wood glue
- ☺ basic collage supplies (see page 12)

∞∞ LE MARIAGE ∞∞

The conceit Meredith Hamilton created for this
watercolor-based collage about marriage is a
wedding cake carousel—a traditional symbol of
romantic love reconfigured to reflect the realities
of life, where relationships are anything but
static. To build the piece, she first inked, then
collaged and painted on top of handmade paper
to create a unified cake shape. Next, she added
stamps, images from vintage books and cards,
smaller watercolors and drawings, and money
fragments. The origins of the merry-go-round
lie in the Crusades, and the name "carrousel"
originally meant "mini war" in French.
Hamilton posits that marriage, too, is a kind of
mini war, with many competing forces at play.
Open "doors" in the cake reveal the mechanism
that powers the carousel, and the bride's hand
(the hand of the artist) holds the control.

Dimensions: 19" in diameter (48 cm) | Artist: Meredith Hamilton

LE MARIAGE ☉

STEPS

1. Paint or draw an unadorned wedding cake. This will be the foundation of your collage, whether you fill it using painting and collage as the artist has done or by collaging on cutout images. Decorate the cake with washes of paint, colorful paper, found or created images, rhinestones, ribbons—whatever works for you. (The artist used pieces of maps and roses made of the leafy drawings on money.)

2. The top layer: If you are making the collage to represent your own marriage, find or make a representation of yourself and your partner. (If you aren't married, rework the image to reflect other important relationships.) This piece is topped with a bridal couple. The groom's head is a drawing of a "blockhead," a wry comment by the artist on the stolid way her husband sometimes relates to people. The bride's face is George Washington's face cut from a U.S. dollar bill and represents financial considerations in life.

3. Layer two contains a second tier of forces, in this case, children. Again, choose whatever is relevant to you—children, friends, career—and find or make appropriate images. The artist has depicted her children riding carousel animals that mirror their personalities: a phoenix, a griffin, and a Pegasus-fish. Their faces are cutout images from Victorian cards.

4. The third tier of the cake is for other significant forces or events: the purchase of a house (shown on a spring, bouncing crazily); friends (represented by animals partying in a swan boat); and career (the artist's desk, looking blank because there's never enough time for art). Alter and embellish your images in creative ways as the artist has done, to show how you feel about these elements in your life.

MATERIALS

- ☉ heavy paper for base (the artist used a handmade paper by Twinrocker)
- ☉ interesting found papers such as money fragments, old stamps, images from old books and maps
- ☉ drawings or photographs of people in your life or representations of those people (from magazines, books, vintage cards)
- ☉ watercolors
- ☉ adhesive: PVA glue
- ☉ basic collage supplies (see page 12)

ENCAUSTIC COLLAGE

PAULA GRASDAL

Encaustic is an ancient technique of painting with pigmented hot wax that produces a luminous and tactile surface. Encaustic paint has three main ingredients: purified beeswax, damar resin (a natural tree resin), and pigment. Encaustic medium, which is beeswax mixed with damar, produces translucent glazes when mixed with the pigmented wax. Encaustic can be cast, carved, scraped, scratched, and embedded with collage materials to produce a wide variety of intriguing results.

Recent availability of premixed encaustic paints and medium has inspired the reemergence of this versatile medium. Artists such as Lynne Perrella (page 181), Tracy Spadafora (page 244), and Cynthia Winika (page 248) incorporate collage elements into their encaustic paintings to great effect. The warm wax acts like an adhesive, and the artist simply encapsulates the absorbent collage materials in the wax. Paper, fabric, photos, leaves, gold leaf, and thread are just a few of the many suitable materials.

BASIC TECHNIQUES

Encaustic technique can be broken down into three basic elements: heating the pigmented wax on a hot palette, painting the hot wax onto an absorbent surface, and fusing each layer with a heat source. For heating the wax, place various colors in small tins on a hot palette (this can be purchased from R&F Handmade Paints or improvised using a Teflon griddle on a hot plate; see Product Resource Guide, page 267) and heat to no more than 220°F (104°C). Using natural bristle brushes (synthetic ones will melt), blend the colors on the hot palette and paint onto the support. Any absorbent surface—a braced wooden panel, watercolor paper, plaster, or "clayboard"—is suitable as a support for wax. Fuse each layer by reheating the wax with a heat gun or tacking iron (this step is important as wax tends to separate into discrete layers). Ventilate well with an exhaust fan next to your work surface as overheated wax fumes can be toxic. If your wax starts smoking, it is too hot—turn down the heat on your palette even if the temperature gauge is at 220°F (104°C).

COLLAGING WITH WAX

Layering delicate paper and wax creates a subtle effect of floating textures and images. Try drawing on translucent rice paper with oil pastel and then embedding it in wax: The paper will seem to disappear, leaving the drawing suspended. Many layers of wax and paper can be added to create a rich surface with lots of depth. Another technique is to cover the support with collage material before adding the encaustic.

EXTENDING THE PROCESS

There are many methods of working with encaustic; here are a few ideas for inspiration. Images can be transferred onto the wax at any stage in the layering process (and no solvents are necessary). Simply place a photocopy of an image face down on cool wax and burnish it with a bone folder. Peel off the paper to reveal a reversed image on the wax. Gilding can be added as a final stage by simply burnishing the metallic leaf with a cotton ball. To embed a line drawing in the surface, incise the wax with a stylus, rub an oil pastel into the lines, and remove excess pastel to reveal the markings. Finally, for an antique effect, layer contrasting encaustic paints on top of each other and, like an archeologist, scrape into the surface to reveal the underlying colors.

For more information on encaustic, see *The Art of Encaustic Painting* by Joanne Mattera.

⊚ EXPRESSING ⊚ DREAMS AND WISHES

There's something about the nature of collage—the juxtaposing of images, the playing with scale, the use of photographically realistic depictions—that has the quality of being both real and unreal at the same time. This in part explains its popularity among the Surrealist artists of the 1930s and 1940s, whose groundbreaking works are the most widely known examples of fine art collage. It also explains why the medium lends itself so well to the exploration of dreams—not just the expression of dreamlike narratives, but the articulation of an artist's wishes and desires. The artists in this chapter do a little of both, and their creations range from concentrated works focused on a single theme to dynamic pieces whose many parts evoke myriad interconnected meanings.

In "Transformation" (page 184), Paula Grasdal explores the theme of change and mutability as expressed through the image of a butterfly, surrounded by sinuous green vines and placed against a patch of vivid sky. Abstract in the manner of a dream, in which a butterfly represents the dreamer, this evocative piece celebrates the transformative possibilities inherent in any significant life change. It also shows us that collages don't have to spell things out to effectively get their meaning across. When you're thinking about how to begin a project, be open to thematic approaches rather than getting bogged down in specific narrative details. As the modernists used to say, sometimes less truly is more.

A project that successfully waxes specific, Kathy Cano-Murillo's "World Traveler's Dream Mobile" (page 193) is a fanciful construction made of ordinary materials: CDs, paper, dowels, ribbon, and beads. A kinetic presentation of twelve miniature collages, each of which represents a country the artist would like to travel to, this intricate mobile embodies the inquisitive energy of the dreamer who wishes to explore the unknown. Pictures of elephants, dancers, drinks, and dragons decorate the vibrant disc surfaces, joining together multiple fantasies about adventure and travel. Another interesting aspect to this piece is that because it is a mobile, it actually moves—a further way to underline the fact that it is about travel and moving around in the world.

In a slightly more surreal vein, Olivia Thomas conjured up a magical doll (page 178) that houses dreams and wishes. With a body made of artfully appliquéd and painted fabric, a photo transfer face (from a vintage photograph), and crochet-hook arms, the doll seems like an amalgamation of the aesthetics of different eras. She carries simple objects in her belly—a key, a heart, coins, and dice—that symbolize her inner desires for wisdom, love, prosperity, and luck. (When making a project like this, choose objects that have special meaning, as they will add potency to the wish.) The dreamy effect of the painted fabric surface makes an effective visual foil to the everyday nature of the found objects, creating a context in which it is easy to believe in their talisman-like powers. Because of the ease with which real items can be incorporated into collages, artists can take advantage of the evocative powers of those objects to create shrine-like artworks in which everyday things can symbolize more complex desires for happiness, artistic fulfillment, or love.

Making use of a range of surrealist effects, Holly Harrison's "Dream House" (page 190) depicts specific wishes and desires for a happy life through a whimsical representation of an ideal house. Liberally sprinkling the picture with under- and oversize images, the artist shows a bird making its nest atop a red house, which has several windows open to reveal specific desires: romance, artistic friends, and fabulous shoes. The smoke curling from the chimney is computer-manipulated sheet music, while (in a nod to René Magritte) silver folk art stars sparkle in a daytime sky. Happy flowers wear human faces, a map of New York covers the roof, and game pieces mark the path to the front door. The key to making a piece like this is that there are no rules—follow your imagination wherever it leads. Just as dream logic creates fantastical scenarios

and disjointed narratives, so does this collage explore the desires of the mind and heart through impossible scale, quirky juxtapositions, and playfully altered imagery.

As demonstrated by the range of projects not just in this chapter but in the book as a whole, collage is an extremely flexible medium. And because it requires an intuitive approach—piecing things together that seem to fit, finding a composition that "feels right"—there are almost no limits to what you might discover or say. As you move your collage elements around on a surface, you'll find that some images seem to "speak" to each other while others retreat into the background, letting themselves be obscured by veils of paint or paper only to assert themselves in the finished product as secret meanings or partially revealed truths. In the same way that a dreamer moves through a dream, piecing together disparate elements until a kind of narrative is born, so does the artist travel through the making of a collage, without fully knowing where he or she is going but confident in the merits of the journey.

⟡ ART DOLL ⟡

*Combining found objects with fabric collage,
stamping, and photo transfer techniques,
Olivia Thomas has shaped a whimsical
personification of her hopes and dreams: A red
and yellow doll with burning desires caged in her
belly, held in place by a simple mesh screen.
By embellishing layers of patterned fabric with
buttons, beads, and wire, Thomas has created a
rich, tactile surface filled with personal symbols.
She also plays with scale and visual contrasts,
combining a vintage photograph face and wiry
crochet-hook arms with a rectangular body to
produce a surrealistic effect.*

Dimensions: 9 ¼" h × 5 ¾" w × 1 ¾" d (23½ cm × 14½ cm × 4½ cm) | Artist: Olivia Thomas

STEPS

1. Paint a piece of muslin, using two to three colors. Add stamp designs or designs made by applying paint with found objects. If you're having trouble starting, establish a color scheme or theme. Anything goes—don't be afraid to try any idea, no matter how outrageous it seems at first.

2. Cut out one doll shape as desired from the muslin and another from a commercial print to use as back and front. Cut out legs and arms (or make them out of found objects, see Step 4). Stuff and sew closed. Use a photo transfer for the face (for this technique, see page 215). Appliqué fabrics onto the doll shape, and add trims and laces, mixing textures and juxtaposing opposites (soft/hard, shiny/dull, etc.). If a sewing machine is not available, sew by hand.

3. Sew closed the doll torso by placing front right sides together, making sure to leave an opening for stuffing. Turn the fabric right side out, stuff with batting, and complete the seam by hand. For a rustic effect, try using rugged whipstitch embroidery.

4. Embellish the body, head, and legs with beads, sequins, wire, buttons, etc. Attach a small screen area and fill it with found objects that symbolize your heart's desires. Sew on the legs and arms. The appendages can be made out of anything you fancy; the artist used old rusted crochet hooks wrapped with wires and beads for arms.

MATERIALS

- ◎ fabrics such as muslin and a printed fabric
- ◎ photo transfer
- ◎ found objects such as a key, heart, coins, dice
- ◎ embellishments such as beads, sequins, trims, lace, buttons, screen
- ◎ stuffing
- ◎ paints
- ◎ oil of wintergreen (for transfers)
- ◎ crayons
- ◎ stamps
- ◎ objects for printing on the fabric
- ◎ pliers
- ◎ wire
- ◎ needle, thread, and sewing machine
- ◎ basic collage supplies (see page 12)

◎ Olivia Thomas's Creativity Tips

The best thing that works for me is that the more I create, the more I create. Making and creating things generates endless ideas for me to try. I keep notebooks of ideas and often refer to them for a jumpstart. I like to pick a theme (love, angst, chaos) and color scheme to get going on projects. Just choose three to five colors and go from there. Let a piece mutate often, changing as it goes, until it has a life of its own.

⊚⊚ CEREMONIAL FIGURE I ⊚⊚

To create an image with the look of an antique icon, Lynne Perrella combined collage with the ancient technique of encaustic painting. She was able to create the aged effect by building up many wax layers over images she applied to the support using photo transfer techniques. With its luminescent colors broken up by lines scratched into the surface, the piece is reminiscent of a stained-glass window on which a talismanic winged figure—a muse or perhaps the artist's creative self—is surrounded by the essential elements of its creativity.

Dimensions: 12" × 9" (30 cm × 23 cm) | Artist: Lynne Perrella

CEREMONIAL FIGURE I ☉

STEPS

1. To begin this project, read about encaustic technique on page 45. Gather images that compel you—dream images or representations of fantasies or goals. Make black-and-white photocopies and use these to make photo transfers onto a piece of printmaking paper (for the solvent transfer technique, see page 215). Apply the transfers so they create a pattern base for the collage.

2. Glue the printmaking paper onto the masonite and weight it overnight. To prevent the first layer of paint from being absorbed into the paper, apply a thin layer of melted beeswax to the surface. Apply multiple layers of encaustic paint to build up a "history," until you are satisfied with the look.

3. Add collage elements by dipping them into encaustic medium and then placing them on the support. Burnish them with a rigid plastic scraper. Be creative in your choice of materials: The artist made the figure's torso and wings from a manila file folder. The androgynous face is an archival image she often uses; it transforms and morphs in novel ways with each new collage.

4. When the elements are all in place, scribe into the wax surface with a sharp tool. Rub dark oil sticks into the markings and wipe away excess color. In this piece, a web of scribed lines enhances the "faux icon" aspect and adds a sense of history and deterioration. You can also use this technique to add words or images that expand or comment upon your theme.

5. Once the collage is fully dry, buff the surface to bring up the warmth of the colors and add sheen.

MATERIALS

- ☉ piece of untempered masonite
- ☉ printmaking paper (the artist used Arches)
- ☉ photocopies of images
- ☉ collage elements such as vintage or handmade papers
- ☉ oil of wintergreen (for transfers)
- ☉ beeswax
- ☉ encaustic paints and medium
- ☉ oil sticks
- ☉ natural bristle brushes
- ☉ scribing tools
- ☉ heated palette (for heating wax)
- ☉ plastic scraper
- ☉ heated spatula
- ☉ basic collage supplies (see page 12)

☉ Lynne Perrella's Creativity Tips

The best way to maintain a constant and lively flow of creativity is to acknowledge our lifelong enthusiasms and use them as an endless reference library. Return to colors, images, themes, quotations, and iconography that have always resonated strongly for you. The artwork done as a result of honoring those enthusiasms is bound to be personal, revealing, and reflective of our true selves.

⧢ TRANSFORMATION ⧣

With its subtle variations in texture and color, Paula Grasdal's ethereal printed rice paper collage gives the impression of being a moving image caught in a single moment. Grasdal achieved the effect by collaging layers of translucent, printed rice papers onto heavier, earth-toned papers, then emphasizing the wrinkled surface of the glued papers with white oil pastel. A monoprint of a butterfly, a symbol of transformation, is set against a background of sinuous growing vines. It's as if the butterfly is emerging from the tangled weeds into an open meadow under a blue sky.

Dimensions: 16" x 15" (41 cm x 38 cm) | Artist: Paula Grasdal

TRANSFORMATION ☺

STEPS

1. This project can be made using any images that inspire you, especially those drawn from nature. Draw images of your choice on sketch paper. Place a piece of Mylar film over the secondary image (in this case, the vine drawing), trace it with a pencil, and cut the shape out with a craft knife. Set aside.

2. Brush water-mixable oil paints diluted with a small amount of water-mixable linseed oil onto the Mylar shape, and place a piece of damp rice paper on top. Cover the back of the paper with a sheet of Mylar film and burnish with a wooden spoon to transfer the image. Repeat several times to create collage materials.

3. To create a monoprint of your primary image (the butterfly), place a small piece of Mylar film over the drawing and paint the image directly onto the film with diluted water-mixable oils. Place the Mylar printing plate, paint side down, on a piece of dampened rice paper, and burnish with the back of a wooden spoon. Let dry.

4. Decide on the general composition of your piece and keep it in mind as you work. Cut a piece of the brown paper to use as backing and collage rice papers to it with diluted PVA. Add layers of the printed papers made in Step 2, tearing some of the papers to create a random background design in selected areas. Let dry. (If desired, coat the surface with diluted glue to emphasize the paper's translucency.) To build up the collage, lightly brush the wrinkled surfaces with gesso; add more printed papers and also gold tissue paper. To create a colorful area like the blue square, paint a section with diluted water-mixable oils, let dry, and highlight the textures with a white oil pastel.

5. Gesso a small piece of brown paper, collage print fragments onto it, and then glue the monoprint made in Step 3 on top. Let dry, then glue into place on the collage.

6. Glue the completed collage to a canvas board cut to size and roll with a brayer to smooth out air bubbles.

MATERIALS

☺ images for inspiration

☺ medium-weight brown paper

☺ assorted translucent rice papers and metallic gold tissue paper

☺ sketch paper

☺ canvas board

☺ Mylar polyester film

☺ gesso

☺ water-mixable oil paints and water-mixable linseed oil (or substitute water-based printing inks)

☺ white oil pastel

☺ wooden spoon

☺ spray bottle

☺ two 9" × 12" (23 cm × 30 cm) pieces of Plexiglas

☺ adhesive: PVA glue

☺ basic collage supplies (see page 12)

TIPS

Vary the density and color of the paint on the secondary shape for a more interesting print (the artist used a palette of olive green, yellow ochre, and brown for the vine). To dampen the rice papers for printing, lightly mist every other sheet and press the papers between two pieces of Plexiglas.

❧ ARCADIA ☙

Inspired by the courtyard gardens of Persian miniatures, Paula Grasdal created a paper collage that embodies her vision of an idyllic sanctuary. To make the layered background, she collaged various rice papers onto printmaking paper. Then she used a monoprinting process and water-based media to embed patterns and textures into the paper, some of which she cut into the arch and tree shapes. The artist was able to make this highly textured, multi-layered collage without a printmaking press by using a Mylar printing plate, absorbent printmaking paper, and a burnishing tool.

Dimensions: 12 ½" × 9" (32 cm × 23 cm) | Artist: Paula Grasdal

ARCADIA ☉

1. Sketch tree and arch designs and set aside. Using a metal ruler as a guide, tear the printmaking paper to size; the artist made 9" × 9" (23 cm × 23 cm) squares. Cut a piece of Mylar film slightly larger than the squares to use as a printing plate.

2. Tear various colored rice papers into fragments. Mix together PVA and paste glue in equal amounts. Use this mixture to collage the fragments to the paper squares. Let dry.

3. Mix the gouache paints with monotype base in colors of your choice. (Tip: Since this process involves overprinting, test how the colors mix when printed on each other.) Lightly brush a color onto the Mylar printing plate, place the plate (paint side down) onto the paper squares, and burnish the back of the plate with a wooden spoon. Varying the colors for contrast, brush paint onto different textures such as cork or wood veneer. Arrange the painted textures on the Mylar plate, place a paper square on top, and gently burnish the back of the paper. Repeat until you have enough paper (you'll need at least four pieces this project).

4. Cut leaf and vine shapes from cork paper, coat them with paint, then print the shapes on translucent rice and tissue papers using the method described above for printing textures. When the paint is dry, collage the rice and tissue paper prints onto the paper squares.

5. Transfer the arch and tree sketches onto the back of two of the printed papers made in Step 3 and cut out the shapes. With PVA, collage the cutouts onto a paper square in a contrasting color, roll with a brayer, and let dry. Cut another square into a strip that will complete the bottom of the collage, and glue all of the pieces to the masonite backing.

VARIATIONS

Create interesting textures by spraying water onto the painted printing plate or by drawing into the wet paint with a dry brush. Instead of a garden, make a monoprint collage that conjures a different ideal place: a beach, a forest, or even a city.

MATERIALS

- ☉ piece of masonite (in desired size)
- ☉ tree and arch designs
- ☉ rice paper in natural and sage colors
- ☉ absorbent printmaking paper (the artist used Arches 88)
- ☉ transfer paper
- ☉ Mylar polyester film
- ☉ gouache paints
- ☉ monotype base
- ☉ textured objects for printing (the artist used cork paper, wood veneer, and mesh)
- ☉ wooden spoon
- ☉ palette knives
- ☉ freezer paper (for paint palettes)
- ☉ adhesives: PVA glue, paste glue
- ☉ basic collage supplies (see page 12)

❧ DREAM HOUSE ❧

Using found paper and digitally altered images, Holly Harrison created a folk art collage about the perfect home. A bird, an image for the soul, represents the artist; it perches atop a red house styled as an advent calendar. In the windows are dreams: at bottom left, an art photo of the artist with friends to show a life filled with art and friendship; at bottom right, a comic book drawing to represent romantic love; and at top left, a cornucopia of funky shoes. Other images include music paper manipulated to look like smoke, flowers with Elvis Presley heads, and cats peeking from behind trees and out of windows.

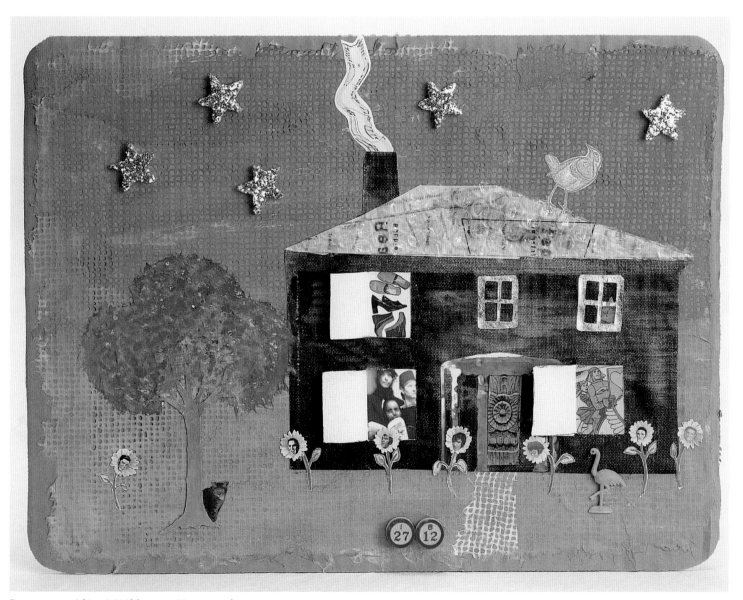

Dimensions: 12" × 16" (30 cm × 41 cm) | Artist: Holly Harrison

DREAM HOUSE ☺

STEPS

1. Cut a piece of cardboard or mat board to a desired size, and coat it on both sides with acrylic medium. Let dry. Paint a sheet of lace paper with colors for your background (the artist painted a grid-patterned sheet with blue and green acrylics to represent sky and grass). Let dry, then adhere to the cardboard base using acrylic medium.

2. Scan a picture of a house into a computer and in Photoshop, size it and add artistic effects; print out on heavy paper. (Alternately, get the size and effect you want using a color photocopier.) To make window frames, apply gold leaf to craft or art paper, let dry, then cut out frames with a craft knife. Adhere the frames onto the house, then make cuts on three sides for the windows you wish to open.

3. Create images for the open windows by culling through magazines, newspapers, comic books, etc. Cut out images that represent all you could wish for in your perfect home.

4. Create or find images to represent other ideals. This piece uses computer-altered images, a map of New York City on the roof covered by bubble wrap, Bingo pieces for the house number, a plastic flamingo, photographs of the artist's cats, a tree made from painted craft and lace papers, and flowers drawn by the artist and collaged with photos.

5. Once you have assembled your materials, lay them out on the background and move them around until you like the composition. Adhere the papers with acrylic medium and the found objects with craft glue. Hang your collage on the wall and watch your dreams come true.

MATERIALS

- cardboard or mat board base
- lace papers in varied patterns
- found papers such as maps, newspapers, comic books, images of a favorite celebrity
- found objects and embellishments
- heavy craft or art paper
- acrylic paints
- imitation gold leaf
- glitter
- digital camera (optional)
- adhesives: acrylic matte medium, craft glue, leaf sizing
- basic collage supplies (see page 12)

⊘⊘ WORLD TRAVELER'S ⊘⊘ DREAM MOBILE

Kathy Cano-Murillo recycled free Internet CDs into a whimsical travel mobile. First, she created mini collages on both sides of six discs and dedicated each one to an exotic place in the world that she would like to visit (or revisit): a Polynesian island, Asia, Mexico, Africa, India, New Orleans, and Europe. The travel imagery ranges from realistic details (a tiny shopping bag and actual coins) to fantasies (images of dragons, masks, and beautiful dancers), uniting disparate parts of the world in one imaginative whole, the way multiple narratives are united through the unique logic of dreaming.

Dimensions: 42" × 22" (107 cm × 56 cm) | Artist: Kathy Cano-Murillo

WORLD TRAVELER'S DREAM MOBILE ☺

STEPS

1. Cover the CDs on both sides with decorative papers and add collage elements as desired. With hot glue, trim the discs with beads. Drill a hole at the top and bottom of each disc.

2. Drill a hole in the center and at both ends of each dowel. Cut two 30" (76 cm) lengths of twine. Thread each through an end hole in the long dowel, leaving 10" (25 cm) dangling. Knot the twine on both sides of the dowel to hold in place. Bring the longer pieces up, knot them together at 10" (25 cm), and tie them onto a ring for hanging. Thread a dangling end through the center hole of each short dowel, securing with knots, to attach the short dowels beneath the longer one.

3. Cut a 5" (13 cm) length of twine. Thread it through the center hole of the long dowel so it hangs down, and secure with knots. Cut four 8" (20 cm) lengths of twine. Thread them through the four end holes in the short dowels so they hang down; secure with knots.

4. With wire cutters, snip eighteen 4" to 5" (10 cm to 13 cm) strips of copper wire. Bend them into decorative S-shaped swirls with needle-nose pliers. Hook the swirls through each hole in each disc. Attach four discs to the short dowels, using a second copper swirl to connect a disc's top swirl to the twine.

5. For the centerpiece, snip an 8" to 10" (20 cm to 25 cm) strip of wire and make a large decorative swirl. Connect two discs together as shown and attach them to the twine dangling at the center, using the large swirl and another tiny one, if needed. Adjust the twine so the central element hangs slightly below the others. Attach ribbons as shown. Trim the tops of all the dowels with beads.

MATERIALS

- 6 CDs
- assorted images, stamps, and tiny trinkets of locations you would like to visit someday
- decorative papers such as stationery or wrapping paper
- 6 to 8 strings of Mardi Gras beads
- colorful glass pebbles
- sixteen 24" (61 cm) strips of brightly colored ribbon
- one 1" (3 cm) dowel, 16" (41 cm) long
- two 1" (3 cm) dowels, 8" (20 cm) long each
- spool of strong, thin twine
- spool of copper wire
- large metal ring (for hanging)
- handheld drill
- wire cutters
- needle-nose pliers
- adhesives: industrial-strength craft glue, hot-glue gun
- basic collage supplies (see page 12)

TIP

Stick with light collage objects. When finished, hang the mobile to check it for balance. If there is tilting, glue colored glass pebbles to discs as needed to correct.

USING SYMBOLS IN COLLAGE

By its very nature, collage encourages intriguing juxtapositions of images and is for this reason an excellent medium for exploring their symbolic meanings. In "Ceremonial Figure I" (page 181), Lynne Perrella turns a simple archival image of a face into something magical and evocative by collaging it onto a winged torso. The same face in any number of different contexts would have a different effect—surreal if perched on a doll's body, sinister if peering out of a dark archway, mysterious if hidden by veils of translucent tissue paper.

Using layers of images or symbols can help build up a narrative about a particular project's theme. In "The Chess Lesson" (page 166), Paula Grasdal uses a chessboard as the base pattern of a collage about her father, who loved the game. Found objects represent game pieces and act as deeper symbols: A metal crown stands not only for the king, but for kingly attributes such as strength of character that the artist associates with her father.

When looking for symbols to use in artwork, one of the richest sources surrounds us: the world we live in. Often without realizing it, we internalize cultural interpretations of elements both natural and constructed. The red rose is for love, the white for purity; a lighthouse offers safety, a tower entrapment and isolation. By tapping into these archetypes, artists can put together a personal lexicon of symbols to use while working. The effective use of symbols is a powerful tool. Some artists, such as Chantale Légaré (pages 151 and 242), create a unique symbol system that alludes to their vision of the world and forms a cohesive body of work.

The box on the following page lists a variety of symbols (some appear in collages in this book) that might be useful to you. Or if you are in search of more inspiration, try thumbing through books that deal with systems of symbols such as alchemy, Tarot, the Kabbalah, hieroglyphics, dream interpretation, numerology, or heraldry.

A Short Lexicon of Symbols

Architecture

Doorway or gate—passage, transition

Fountain—eternal life; in dreams: secrets of the unconscious

House—psyche, dwelling of soul

Roof—feminine, sheltering principle

Stairs—steps in spiritual development, passage of life to death to immortality

Wall—strength, containment

Window—eye of the soul, consciousness, perception

Colors

Black—in West: death and mourning; Hindus: time; Egyptians: rebirth and resurrection

Blue—spirit, intellect; poet Wallace Stevens used it to symbolize imagination

Brown—earth, autumn

Gold—perfection, knowledge

Gray—penitence, humility

Green—life, nature; can be jealousy

Orange—flames, pride, ambition

Pink—flesh, emotions, heart

Purple—royalty, pride, truth

Red—life force, blood; Chinese: good luck; also courage, love

Silver—linked to moon, magic; Christianity: purity, chastity

Violet—most mystical color; also sorrow and mourning

White—purity, perfection, sacredness; Asia: color of mourning

Yellow—faithlessness, betrayal; when associated with sun: illumination, light, and intellect

Human body

Foot—balance, freedom of movement

Footprint—leaving one's mark

Hands—open, palms up: welcome; folded: submission; raised to head: thought

Heart—love, compassion

Nature

Bat—darkness and chaos in some cultures; Chinese: good luck, longevity

Bees—immortality

Bird—the soul; can represent angels

Butterfly—metamorphosis, rebirth

Crow—Western: ill omen; Native American: the creative principle; African: guide, messenger of the gods

Dragonfly—regeneration, change; Chinese: instability

Egg—origins, beginnings, hope, immortality

Electricity—creative energy

Entwined snakes—dual creative forces (good and evil)

Forest—darkness, chaos, uncertainty; in psychology: the unconscious

Garden—paradise

Griffin—vigilance, vengeance, wisdom

Lotus—ancient Asian symbol for enlightenment

Moon—female sign, resurrection, cyclical nature of things

Scarab—Egyptian symbol of renewal and regeneration

Sun—male sign, active, creative energy

Orchid—Chinese symbol of perfection

Pegasus—speed, desire to fly

Phoenix—immortality; also gentleness

Pineapple—hospitality

Salmon—Celtic symbol of prophecy and inspiration

Tree of Life—perfect harmony

Objects

Anchor—stability, safety

Cup—symbol of feminine realm

Hourglass—mortality, passage of time

Key—power to open things, symbol of wisdom

Mirror—reflection, self-knowledge

Thread—life, human destiny

Shapes

Circle—infinity, eternity

Concentric circles—the cosmos

Spiral—vortex of energy (masculine and feminine); in dreams: growth, need for change

Square—dependability, honesty, safety; Hindu: order, balance of opposites

Triangle—the trinity; pointing up: ascent to heaven (male principle); pointing down: grace descending (female principle)

For more on symbols and their meanings, see *The Encyclopedia of Dreams* by Rosemary Ellen Guiley, *The Illustrated Book of Signs and Symbols* by Miranda Bruce-Mitford, and *The Secret Language of Symbols* by David Fontana.

⊚ INSPIRED BY ⊚ NATURE

BECAUSE OF THE PROMINENT use in collage of printed materials and its presence in urban art movements such as Dadaism, Surrealism, and Cubism, we don't always associate this medium with nature or the natural world. Much of what comes to mind when we think "collage" is characterized by the use of symbols, advertising images, typefaces, newspaper clippings, and the like. But there was also an earlier form of collage, when Victorian gentlewomen with time on their hands made elaborate paper constructions layered with flowers, butterfly wings, and feathers. And closer to this century, there's the notable use of sand, leaves, bark, and other natural materials by such painters as Jean Dubuffet and Max Ernst, as well as the iconoclast Joseph Cornell's visual references to astronomy and his longtime fascination with birds.

Just as the advertising images and pop-culture references of the urban aesthetic connect viewer and artist to a whole cultural dimension, natural materials link us to a world of symbols and archetypes that have meaning across many cultures. A branch might represent a tree and symbolize the tree of life. A lotus is not only a beautiful flower, but it is the Eastern symbol of enlightenment. A moonstone is a stone, but as a "tiny moon" it also taps into the many myths and associations that the moon carries across cultures: feminine power, the mystery of creation, cycles of life and death. The artists whose works are in this chapter, whether they use organic materials or simply take their inspiration from nature, all play with the symbolic meanings that are attached to the items or images they use. For example, in "Shhh…" (page 203), Sandra Salamony uses an actual speckled egg along with photocopied images of the egg, and so provides us with both the object and an abstraction of the object. In a sense, she invites us into her process by making an almost casual reference to how art (or artifice) can alter our perceptions of what we see in the world.

The artist who uses nature as his or her starting point, whether as a source of materials or of inspiration, will inevitably end up commenting in some way on the relationship between humanity and nature. Amy Kitchin's "Lilies of the Valley" (page 212), with its fragile bird's nest holding a snake-like fishing lure, hints at an uneasy coexistence of people and the natural world, where a place of refuge gives shelter to a hunter's discarded tool. Offering a radically different take, Karen Michel's "Urban Birdsong"(page 209) shows wise-eyed, singing birds that have adapted to the limitations of their urban environment. Her piece celebrates the power of nature and its ability to regenerate and flourish, even under extreme conditions.

Organically inspired or constructed collages and assemblages reflect another human creation: the garden, a part of nature that has been altered by the human hand and imagination. You might model a piece after a walled medieval garden, an elaborate maze or a simple Zen rock garden. Paula Grasdal created "Secret Garden" (page 200) using images of botanical fragments, lattice screens, a "lost" key, and a patinaed archway, and offers us a fleeting glimpse into an opulent, forgotten courtyard. Though we're always trying to tame nature and impose order on it, once neglected, things revert back to wildness and disorder.

If you watch children outside, you quickly realize that the urge to collect objects is a powerful, inborn one. Shells and sea glass at the beach, small rocks, flowers, and colorful leaves in a garden—these items quickly fill their hands and pockets. And what could be more natural when you find an abandoned bird's nest than to take it home and put it in a shoebox for safekeeping? So we begin to make our first assemblages, which later at school become more formal dioramas, complete with themes and lots of glue.

These early memories of collecting and creating are something we can bring to the making of nature collages and assemblages. Additionally, working with natural materials is satisfying on a visceral level. When we handle feathers, twigs, shells, or sand, we experience ourselves as part of the natural world. And using an actual flower in place of a painted or drawn one creates an immediate link between the art, the viewer, and nature. These are things that are already familiar to us, yet in collage we see them anew through the artist's eyes.

Nature also provides a rich world of color and texture from which an artist can draw inspiration. Try taking the colors from a single rock or a field of flowers as the palette for a collage and you'll discover unimaginable color combinations and hues. Or use the textured surfaces of tree bark and heavily veined leaves to make rubbings for printed-paper collages. There's no end to the variety you'll find in nature, and the challenge is figuring out creative ways to make use of that abundance.

The collage artist who works with (or from) natural materials creates a macrocosm that is a miniature reflection of our world, with one important difference—it can have its own set of rules. In your created world, you can subvert or ignore the laws of nature, letting water exist above sky or letting water and fire occupy the same space. Playing with scale allows large flowers to tower over tiny human figures or stars and dragonflies to coexist. In your world-within-a-box, birds can wear haloes, gardens can keep secrets, and the seasons can be held in permanent suspension. The only limitations, really, are the boundaries of your imagination and the strength of your glue.

When you are foraging for materials outside, whether at the beach or in a forest or meadow, harvest responsibly. Scavenge bark and twigs from the ground rather than living trees, pick flowers only where they grow in abundance (or buy them fresh at a florist or dried at a craft store), and avoid endangered plants. Never take a seemingly unused bird's nest with you in spring—it just might be someone's home.

✤ SECRET GARDEN ✤

For this nature collage, Paula Grasdal combined layers of rice paper, mesh, and cutout paper shapes to create the impression of a light–filled garden glimpsed through a doorway. A single tree graces the site and from its branches hangs a mysterious key, possibly a symbolic reference to the Tree of Knowledge. Insects and plants (tinted photocopies integrated through washes of acrylics) hover nearby. The layers tell a story about making the piece but also convey the idea of a hidden garden, transformed by years of growth and neglect. Perhaps the key will unlock the secrets of its past.

Dimensions: 12" × 9" (30 cm × 23 cm) | Artist: Paula Grasdal

SECRET GARDEN ◎

1. If there's a tree you climbed as a child or a garden you once loved, you can capture the memory in this collage. Start by drawing tree and vine shapes on the heavyweight paper; cut them out using a craft knife and self-healing mat; set aside. Fold a piece of mesh (the size of your masonite) in half lengthwise and cut an arch or other framing shape. Coat it with instant-rust patina and let dry.

2. Trace the arch onto patterned rice paper and cut out. Collage the paper arch to a piece of backing paper using acrylic medium; roll with a brayer and let dry. Arrange torn pieces of rice paper and tinted photocopies on the backing paper as desired, allowing the arch to frame them. Collage the papers on and let dry. Integrate the paper fragments with washes of diluted acrylics, letting each layer dry before applying more paint. Add a sense of depth by dry-brushing gesso onto raised areas to emphasize the textures. For an aged effect, sand parts of the collage once it is dry.

3. Paint the tree and vine cutouts with layers of metallic gold acrylic and a light topcoat of dry-brushed gesso. Glue them to the collage and roll with a brayer.

4. Brush craft glue on the back of the mesh arch and attach it to the paper one, framing the tree. The subtle patterns of the underlying rice paper will show through the patinaed mesh. Highlight areas of the archway with touches of metallic gold paint.

5. Attach the collage to a masonite backing with PVA, roll with a brayer, then coat the back of the masonite with glue to prevent warping. Let dry.

6. Paint a small rectangle of mesh gold and attach it where desired with craft glue; affix the key on top with the industrial-strength glue. Paint the unfinished frame with diluted gesso; sand when dry for a distressed finish. Mount the collage in the frame.

VARIATION

Coat the tree and the area under the mesh archway with imitation gold leaf to create the effect of a medieval icon.

MATERIALS

- ◎ piece of masonite (in desired size)
- ◎ unfinished pine frame
- ◎ heavyweight paper (for background support and the cut-paper shapes)
- ◎ assorted rice papers
- ◎ photocopies of insects and plants
- ◎ rusted key or other found object
- ◎ fiberglass door-screen mesh
- ◎ rust patina kit
- ◎ acrylic paints in assorted colors including metallic gold
- ◎ gesso
- ◎ adhesives: acrylic gel medium, PVA glue, craft glue, industrial-strength craft glue
- ◎ basic collage supplies (see page 12)

◉◉ SHHH… ◉◉

The images of an egg, a butterfly, and a child encapsulate the themes of incubation and transformation in this collage. Photoshop let Sandra Salamony manipulate a butterfly scan into color separations, which she printed onto transparency paper and sandwiched between glass. She also printed scanned photos onto vellum and photocopied an egg in color. Even with its reliance on technology, this piece has a predominantly organic feel, which Salamony established by collaging tea-stained papers and pressed flowers onto wood panels and setting them in an antiqued wooden box. The panels are moveable, symbolizing the many ways in which development can occur.

Dimensions: 8" × 10" (20 cm × 25 cm) | Artist: Sandra Salamony   Butterfly photo: Scott Brown

SHHH … ☺

STEPS

1. Stain an unfinished shadow box walnut, and antique it using soft white acrylic paint, moss green glaze, and tinted finishing wax (to seal). Once dry, sand along the edges to expose stain.

2. To make the glass tile: Scan a photo of a butterfly. In Photoshop, convert the image to CMYK and separate the channels into four images that will print in each color. Print onto transparency paper. (Alternatively, use a color photocopier to approximate the effect.) Trim to 3" (8 cm) squares, remove the cyan, and sandwich the remaining images between the three glass squares with the black and magenta together and the yellow on its own. Wrap with adhesive copper tape.

3. To make the front panels: Cut two 3¼" × 8" (8½ cm × 20 cm) panels of basswood. Use glue and collage medium to attach decorative papers, pressed flowers, and photocopies to the panels. Stain the papers with tea, and mottle with moss green glaze. To secure the butterfly tile, use brass escutcheon pins (aged in darkening solution). To attach the hollow egg, use a hot-glue gun.

4. To make the see-through panel: Using wire cutters, trim a 4" × 8" (10 cm x 20 cm) piece of hardware cloth. Print a photo on vellum (use a laser printer) and collage it onto the hardware cloth. Let dry. Print a color scan of a flower or other image on transparency paper. Trim to size and staple it to the wire frame.

5. To make the SHHH panel: Cut a 4" × 8" (10 cm × 20 cm) panel of basswood. Print a photo on vellum and collage it onto the panel. Let dry. Stamp letters using the wooden type and sepia calligraphy ink. Wrap hardware cloth or other embellishment around the bottom.

6. Assembling: Paint the ¼" × ¼" (½ cm × ½ cm) basswood strips with soft white acrylic paint and cut into eight 8" (20 cm) lengths. Glue into the box to create runners at top and bottom, incorporating the panels as you go and leaving room for them to slide. The two back panels share the same runners. Add the type if desired (as shown).

MATERIALS

- 8" × 10" (20 cm × 25 cm) shadow box
- two 4" × 24" (10 cm × 61 cm) basswood panels, ¼" (½ cm) thick
- three ¼" × ¼" (½ cm × ½ cm) basswood strips, 24" (61 cm) long
- wooden type to spell a word or sound
- embellishments such as a speckled egg, pressed flowers, photographs
- assorted papers (the artist used wall paper, transparency paper, cream vellum, natural bark paper, and acid-free tissue paper)
- hardware cloth
- three 3" (8 cm) squares of glass, 1/16" (⅛ cm) thick
- self-adhesive copper metal tape
- walnut stain
- soft white acrylic paint
- moss green glaze
- tinted finishing wax
- sepia calligraphy ink
- brewed black tea
- four brass escutcheon pins and brass-darkening solution
- handheld saw
- adhesives: PVA glue, hot-glue gun, collage medium (an equal mix of acrylic matte medium and water)
- basic collage supplies (see page 12)

✆ ✆ STRATA ✆ ✆

*This collage combines the techniques of frottage
(taking a rubbing of a textured surface to create
a design) and tissue-paper lamination to create
layers of subtle color and texture. To establish the
delicate color fields, Paula Grasdal tinted white
tissue paper with water-mixable oil paints. She
then encapsulated images of ammonites between
layers of painted tissue, creating the look of
fossilized impressions found in the earth's strata.
The difference is that the translucency of the
paper allows us to look within the layers to see
the treasures buried there.*

Dimensions: 6½" × 13" (17 cm × 33 cm) | Artist: Paula Grasdal

STRATA ⊚

STEPS

1. Cut out a selection of photocopied images and lightly tint them with diluted water-mixable oil paint. Place the white craft tissue over leaf skeletons (or other natural objects) and rub with the side of a wax crayon to create textures. Make several rubbings.

2. Place the rubbings on freezer paper and tint them with diluted water-mixable oil paints (the artist used yellow ochre, cadmium orange, phthalo green, and olive green). Leave some rubbings untinted for use in Step 5.

3. Cut two pieces of white craft tissue (the size you will want the collage to be) and place one on a piece of freezer paper. Coat it with diluted PVA glue using a wide foam brush, and place the second piece on top, flattening air bubbles with a brayer. Let dry.

4. Rip the tinted tissue into manageable sizes. Working a section at a time, brush glue onto the prepared backing tissue and press the ripped pieces onto the glued area. Let dry.

5. Glue your chosen images in place and paint diluted glue on the central portion of the collage, leaving a 1" (3 cm) border. Place a white piece of tissue onto this central area and roll with a brayer. Layer several untinted rubbings on the surface so that they overlap the images. Coat the collage with diluted glue to make the tissue more translucent.

6. When the tissue has dried, highlight surface textures with oil pastels and define the outside edges with gold oil pastel.

VARIATIONS

Encase metallic thread or natural materials such as feathers between the tissue layers. Create a memory collage by substituting copies of family photographs for the fossils. If you wish, you can use liquid acrylics and matte medium instead of the water-mixable oil paints and PVA glue.

MATERIALS

⊚ white craft tissue

⊚ photocopies of fossils

⊚ leaf skeletons (for rubbings)

⊚ water mixable oil paints in various colors

⊚ oil pastels

⊚ black wax crayon

⊚ freezer paper

⊚ adhesive: PVA glue

⊚ basic collage supplies (see page 12)

⊙⊙ URBAN BIRDSONG ⊙⊙

*A mixed-media collage mounted on wood,
Karen Michel's colorful piece celebrates the
adaptability of nature. Using water-soluble oil
pastels, watercolor pencils, and gesso, she created
four brightly pigmented landscapes with
scratched-away city skylines. These—rather than
the blue-sky background—are home to birds
sporting oddly human eyes (in fact, cutouts from
magazines). By adapting themselves to their city
home, these humanized birds, with their shiny
paper hearts and painted haloes, are able to
survive, even thrive, in the urban world.*

Dimensions: 17 ½" × 12" (44 cm × 30 cm) | Artist: Karen Michel

URBAN BIRDSONG ⑨

STEPS

1. Cut a piece of wood to size and prime it with a generous layer of gesso. Once the gesso is dry, apply water-soluble oil pastels, working well into the surface with a wet paintbrush. Add more water and pastel as needed to get desired surface.

2. Cut the paper to prepare the individual collages. There are no limits to the possibilities this project offers: The work can be made of many small collages, a few larger ones, or one big one. You can also use as many eyelets as you like.

3. For each collage, prepare the paper surface with a layer of gesso. Once the gesso is dry, begin drawing. Sketch with a pencil first and then work the background with various colors using water-soluble oil pastels. Scratch into the background to achieve desired effects. For the bird's eyes, the artist used human eyes cut out of magazines, which she applied to the surface with acrylic medium.

4. Once the collages are complete, insert eyelets into the corners. Lay the collages out on top of the wood with a dab of acrylic medium on the back to hold them in place. Once you are happy with the layout, gently hammer a short nail into the wood through each eyelet. You can now go back into the wood background and rework the surface or add additional composition elements to the work.

MATERIALS

- ⑨ sheet of wood (in desired size)
- ⑨ paper for individual collages
- ⑨ magazine clippings
- ⑨ water-soluble oil pastels
- ⑨ watercolor pencils
- ⑨ gesso
- ⑨ eyelet pliers and small eyelets
- ⑨ short nail tacks
- ⑨ adhesive: acrylic matte medium
- ⑨ basic collage supplies (see page 12)

TIP

Avoid acrylic gesso: The finish dries glossy and makes it more difficult to work pigments into; sandable hard gesso works best. When working large areas with water-soluble pastels, dip the pastel in water and work it from its side across your surface, dipping as often as needed. Acrylic matte medium will seal and make your collage re-workable without a shiny, high-gloss glare.

⤬⤬ LILIES OF THE VALLEY ⤬⤬

Made of natural found objects, an old fishing lure, and a graphite drawing by the artist, this piece was inspired by Amy Kitchin's childhood memories of growing up in a house surrounded by woods, hills, creeks, and bridges. Deceptively simple in its wooden box decorated with dried flowers, the assemblage juxtaposes the natural (a cozy bird's nest) with the manufactured (a wooden fishing lure) to create a sense of tension. Though the effect is of a harmonious whole, we quickly realize that the snake-like fishing lure has found its way into a place meant for refuge and safety.

Dimensions: 15" h × 5" w × 3" d (38 cm x 13 cm × 8 cm) | Artist: Amy Kitchin

LILIES OF THE VALLEY ☉

1. The artist began with a small graphite drawing done on vellum. Find or make something similar. If you have an image you like and want to transfer it onto vellum, you can use a photocopier. Tearing the edges of the drawing will create a sense that it is a fragment of a memory. To prevent smudging, spray fixative on the drawing.

2. Paint the inside and outside of the box, and then adhere the vellum drawing inside using acrylic medium as both glue and a sealant. Because vellum is translucent, you can also collage leaves or other flat objects underneath.

3. Arrange and glue the various found objects to the inside and outside of the box. If you use a bird's nest as one of your found objects, glue a small square of paper onto the bottom to help preserve the structure before gluing the whole thing into the box.

4. To adhere objects to the nest (such as the fishing lure), use a thin wire instead of glue, which will mat the nest. Make a tiny hole in the back of the box with a hammer and nail. Wrap the wire around the lure, and then thread both ends of the wire through the back of the nest and through the hole. Secure the lure to the box by twisting together the ends of the wire.

5. Add dried flowers, wood pieces, and other embellishments as desired, inside and out.

MATERIALS

- ☉ old wooden box
- ☉ found natural objects such as willow branches, a bird's nest, bay leaves, dried flowers
- ☉ found wooden objects (the artist used pieces from a drying rack and an old fishing lure)
- ☉ vellum
- ☉ acrylic paints
- ☉ fixative spray
- ☉ wire
- ☉ adhesives: acrylic matte medium, PVA glue (such as Sobo), industrial-strength craft glue
- ☉ basic collage supplies (see page 12)

TIP

Be creative and thoughtful about the way you adhere or attach objects into a space. You can sew objects into place, attach them with hinges, or wrap and tie them with string, wire or fabric. Glue isn't always the best option.

PHOTO TRANSFERS FOR COLLAGE

PAULA GRASDAL

Vintage photographs, memorabilia, and old etchings add character to a collage project, but what if you want to preserve these objects? Photo transfers produce intriguing results and are a way to incorporate one-of-a-kind items in a project without parting with precious originals. Almost any image can be photocopied and transferred onto an absorbent surface such as canvas, silk, paper or spackling using solvent or acrylic medium.

SOLVENT TRANSFERS

Solvent transfers have a dreamlike quality, which lends itself beautifully to memory collages. This technique works best on natural fibers such as paper, silk, or cotton and is effective on absorbent surfaces such as spackling or joint compound. To make a solvent transfer with nontoxic oil of wintergreen (available at pharmacies), place a photocopy of your image face down on paper or fabric and secure it with tape. Dip a cotton swab in the oil and coat the back of the photocopy. Burnish with a bone folder to transfer the image, and lift a corner of the paper to check its progress (repeat if necessary). Experiment with solvent transfers on sheer silk organza, craft tissue paper, and rice paper to use when layering images in your collages. Overlays of translucent images can introduce a mysterious and subtle atmosphere.

ACRYLIC MEDIUM TRANSFERS

Acrylic medium transfers produce a crisp image and can be tinted with diluted acrylic paints. As this process involves water, you'll need to use a fabric or watercolor-paper support. Brush a thin layer of acrylic matte medium onto a fresh black-and-white photocopy, set aside, and brush medium onto the fabric. Place the coated photocopy image side down on the coated fabric, and smooth out air bubbles with a brayer. Let dry for 24 hours, and then soak the joined fabric and paper in tepid water until the paper becomes soft. Gently abrade the paper with a sponge to reveal your image, now in reverse, on the fabric. Tint as desired with paints or inks.

COLOR TRANSFERS

Effective color transfers can be made with a color ink-jet printout and acrylic matte medium. Print out a scanned image or a digital-photo collage. Coat the printout and the support with acrylic medium and follow the directions above. When done on tumbled marble tiles or plaster-coated paper, this technique produces an effect that is reminiscent of fresco painting.

Heat transfer paper is a fast and easy way to adhere color images to fabric or heavy paper. With a color photocopier, copy an image or design on the transfer paper. Trim the paper to size and iron, image side down, onto the support using the manufacturer's instructions for heat settings and time. Peel off the backing paper to reveal the design.

For examples of transfer techniques, see pages 166, 178, and 256. For information about manipulating photocopies for collage, see *The Art and Craft of Collage* by Simon Larbalestier.

CREATING VISUAL MEMOIRS

WHEN YOU REMEMBER a place or an event, it's not just the visual picture that comes to mind. The scent of freshly cut grass, the feel of the sun on your shoulders, the sound of a lawn sprinkler off in the distance—when these fragments of sensory information come together, they build a more complete and vivid memory of a summer day. In the same way, the collage artist takes fragments in hand— a section of a map, old photographs, scraps of joss paper— and joins them to create an evocative whole. One might say no subject and medium could be more ideally suited.

Because of the distinct differences in purpose and approach in the making of, say, a scrapbook, and the making of a memory collage, we decided to replace the more commonly used description "memory keeping" with "visual memoir." The scrapbook maker seeks to commemorate an event as it occurred, using ephemera such as menus, pressed flowers, ticket stubs, and photographs to faithfully preserve a memory. The collage artist seeks instead to recall the essence of an event, capture its mood or re-create its ambiance. And quite likely the artist will even take liberties, such as replacing people's heads with those of animals or playing with scale and color, abandoning straight storytelling in favor of communicating a personal vision.

Unlike artists working in other media who create representations (whether abstract or realistic) of objects in their work, the collage artist can use the actual object in a piece. This is a great advantage for visual memoir, in that an object can itself act as a sort of trigger of sensory memory. For example, in "Tuscan Memory Box" (page 218), Paula Grasdal includes an old metal key (located on the inside of the box lid, see photo inset, page 220) in a work that features numerous images of porticos and gates. Not only does this play on the conceit of a key unlocking the door to memory, but the key itself is tangible, rust and all, evoking memories of other keys one might have held or seen. Looking at the collage, you not only take in the portal imagery, but you almost feel the weight of the key in the palm of your hand; by integrating the actual object, Grasdal creates a simple and direct connection between the viewer and her work.

Additionally, old objects are just that—old. In the nicks and blemishes they carry, we see evidence of time that has passed. These objects can connect the artist and viewer with another time and place. Much of the fun in working with found objects is in playing with them, deciphering their stories, imagining them in other contexts, and bringing something of that to your collage. In "Livonia" (page 224), Carol Owen uses many found objects, among them a tarnished silver spoon. By leaving the spoon intact, she both preserves and makes use of its particular past; additionally, she allows the spoon's patina of age to lend the piece a more general historic feel.

What does this all mean for the collage artist? Well, first of all, it means you're not going to want to throw out nifty old clutter that could be put to good use in your artwork. When the spring-cleaning urge hits, toss any items that seem promising into a shoebox or other container (some artists keep their stashes in meticulously labeled boxes). Hang onto keys, interesting postcards, greeting cards or valentines from friends, photos of events and people important to you, books (damaged ones are great for taking apart), maps, toys (even broken ones), games (the pieces can be used separately), bits of fabric, ticket stubs, programs—really, anything that catches your fancy.

It also means you'll probably find yourself scouring yard sales and junky antiques stores. If something surprises you or makes you smile, grab it. If you find a game you played as a kid, an ad for medicine your grandmother took or a headless doll that's strangely fascinating, buy it. Old photographs are priceless treasures—look for out-of-date fashions, remarkable faces, interesting details that grab your attention. Ann Baldwin uses photographs to great effect in "The Way We Were" (page 221), relying not only on the clothing style and body stance of the people to tell a story, but on the black-and-white imagery, which instantly suggests the past.

Where you can't use old objects themselves, you can still create an aura of age or invoke the past by using techniques such as applying color washes to veil photographs, layering tissue paper to add a sense of mystery, or borrowing the sepia tones from old photos or the washed-out palettes of old Polaroids. Scratching surfaces, adding crackle medium, and crumpling papers are also ways to add the appearance of age.

Finally, try not to over-tell your story—mimic memory's elusiveness by partially hiding images under paint, paper or other images, and emphasizing the jagged edges, the fragmented nature of broken toys or other found objects. Memory is, in essence, romantic—it edits our experience of events as they really occurred, of journeys as they were actually lived—often leaving us with only half-glimpsed fragments, whose power is in their mystery. Collage allows us to compose visual memoirs that reveal specifics of a time gone by or a person loved without abandoning the allure of the mysterious that lets art, and the artist, flourish.

❦ TUSCAN MEMORY BOX ❦

To conjure up her past travels in Tuscany, Paula Grasdal mounted four small collages onto canvas board and housed them inside an elegantly transformed cigar box featuring a veneer of Italian maps, patterned vellum, and paint. An image of a door on the lid entices you to open the box and enter her Tuscan homage, which she pieced together using color photocopies of photographs and found ephemera. Images of porticos, statuary, and stucco houses were given an aura of age and mystery by adding layers of translucent paper and washes of diluted paint. Scraps of joss paper add a golden glow, perhaps reflecting the way in which nostalgia often gilds our memories of a favorite place.

Dimensions: 9¼" h × 5¾" w × 1¾" d (23½ cm × 14½ cm × 4½ cm) | Artist: Paula Grasdal

TUSCAN MEMORY BOX ☺

STEPS

1. Lightly sand the cigar box and wipe clean. Rip the map into manageable pieces and collage it onto the outside of the box using acrylic gel medium. Burnish wrinkles with the back of a spoon and let dry. Paint with watered-down white gouache.

2. Line the box interior with decorative paper. Cut the patterned vellum to size and collage it to the top of the lid. Paint around the edges with metallic gold paint.

3. Cut out four canvas-board rectangles to fit inside the box and a smaller one for on the lid. Select color photocopies and other collage materials such as stamps, map fragments, and tickets. Arrange the materials on each panel until you like the effect, but do not adhere. Collage on a background layer of decorative paper. Add layers of torn photocopies, ephemera, and torn tracing paper onto the background paper. Let dry. Repeat for the smaller collage, incorporating some of the patterned vellum. Seal the collages with polyurethane.

4. Cover the backs of the four larger collages with decorative paper (the artist used joss paper squares). Paint the edges with metallic paint. Let dry, then seal with polyurethane.

5. Using craft glue, attach the small collage to the box lid. Lightly sand the outside of the box to create an aged effect. Cut a photocopy to fit inside the picture frame and collage it to the inside of the box lid. Affix a rusted key or other found object to the photocopy with epoxy, then assemble the frame and glue it over the photo and key. Place the collages inside the box.

VARIATION

Attach the collages together with ribbon to create an accordion folding "book." Collage color copies onto the outside of a box to create a unique container for found objects collected on your travels.

MATERIALS

- ☺ cigar box
- ☺ canvas board
- ☺ map of a place that's special to you
- ☺ color photocopies of photographs of that place
- ☺ ephemera such as stamps, tickets, brochures
- ☺ decorative papers (the artist used gold joss paper, beige tracing paper, patterned vellum, and cork paper)
- ☺ small gold picture frame with glass
- ☺ rusted metal key or other found object
- ☺ metallic gold acrylic paint
- ☺ white gouache paint
- ☺ matte polyurethane
- ☺ adhesives: acrylic matte medium, acrylic gel medium, epoxy, craft glue
- ☺ basic collage supplies (see page 12)

⟲⟳ THE WAY WE WERE ⟲⟳

This collage is a combination of scanned photographs and acrylic paints on canvas and was created by Ann Baldwin in memory of her father. Though painted with a loose, easy style, it has a formal feel, established by her choice and placement of photographs. The central image is of her father standing at military attention behind his children. Instead of a joint parental portrait, she used two photos, emphasizing the separateness with a barrier of blue paint. All of the photos are partially veiled with colored glazes, as if we are seeing the family's past through the veil of the artist's perception. Finally, at top left, Baldwin has included an extract from a letter she wrote to her parents as a child. The style is formal and the handwriting neat, indicative of her desire to please them.

Dimensions: 12" × 12" (30 cm × 30 cm) | Artist: Ann Baldwin

STEPS

1. Collect photographs, letters, and meaningful elements to use in your collage. Scan everything into a computer and print out on acid-free paper. Allow the printouts to dry thoroughly for a day. (You can also substitute color photocopies.) Arrange the images and handwritten text on the canvas until you find a placement that pleases you. Adhere with acrylic matte medium and smooth with a brayer.

2. Tear the corrugated cardboard into strips and use them to provide a partial frame for the main photograph.

3. Cover the entire canvas with a layer of matte medium. This will enable you to scratch back into subsequent paint layers without damaging the collaged elements.

4. With a clean brush, "veil" the photos with translucent buff paint. Let dry.

5. Use the acrylic paints to thinly glaze the blank areas of the canvas, cardboard, and parts of the photos, making sure to dry each layer thoroughly before applying the next. The paint should be put on very freely. You might like to add personal thoughts or messages by brushing on an opaque layer of the buff paint and etching in words with the end of the brush while the paint is still wet. Let dry, then apply further transparent glazes of paint. When you have finished, paint the sides of the canvas with black gesso.

6. If desired, brush thick gold paint on the "peaks" of the corrugated cardboard. Finally, apply a layer of gloss medium as a last step to help preserve the photos from the effects of sunlight and to give the painting a light varnish.

MATERIALS

- ☺ 12" × 12" (30 cm × 30 cm) gessoed canvas on heavy stretcher bars, 1¼" (3½ cm) deep
- ☺ reprinted or photocopied photographs
- ☺ handwritten text or letter
- ☺ acid-free paper
- ☺ white corrugated cardboard (craft type or recycled)
- ☺ fluid acrylics in transparent yellow oxide, crimson, gray, and buff
- ☺ tube paint in deep gold
- ☺ black gesso
- ☺ adhesives, acrylic matte meddium, acrylic gel medium
- ☺ basic collage supplies (see page 12)

☺ Ann Baldwin's Creativity Tips

Do more than one collage at the same time. Decide that one is "real" and the other is just messing around. This relieves the pressure of getting it right— and you'll be surprised how often the play collage turns out well. If you become stumped, run an errand, have lunch, and return to your work with fresh eyes. I place my problem paintings in odd corners of the house, where I come across them unexpectedly. In that split second I can view them objectively and often see what needs fixing.

❧❧ LIVONIA ❧❧

Embellished with a wide variety of collage
elements such as cancelled stamps, feathers,
shells, a tarnished silver spoon, buttons, maps,
and photocopies of vintage photographs, this
spirit house strongly evokes a sense of history and
place. Always on the lookout for interesting
faces, Carol Owen uses found photographs
prominently in her work. Rather than portraying
specific personal memories, she explores the
themes of family and memories of home in a
more general, universal way. By glazing over the
photos with a color wash, she integrates them
with the background; in this way, they look
almost like the memories of the people portrayed.

Dimensions: 14" h × 12" w × 4" d (36 cm × 30 cm × 10 cm) | Artist: Carol Owen

STEPS

1. Cut out the foam core to desired shapes (this project is essentially two boxes and a series of lean-tos). Paint both sides of the core with acrylic medium; this will prevent warping. Cover both sides of the core pieces with rice paper, smoothing out carefully to avoid puckering. Let dry.

2. Assemble the spirit house using the textile glue. Paint freely with acrylic paints. Let dry.

3. Arrange photos and other paper ephemera as desired, then glue down using the textile glue. While arranging the pictures, think about their relationship to each other as well as their placement in the context of the whole. This collage opens to reveal a regal baby at its center, sitting beneath a sun with button rays, on what appears to be a throne of maps, and holding a scepter-like spoon across its knees. The artist has provided a delightful surprise for anyone who looks inside the box.

4. Glaze over the surface with thin washes of the acrylics and blot. Go over edges of the collage elements and the house with metallic paints or pencils.

5. Embellish with small objects, gluing them in place with craft glue. Use the embellishments to draw attention to certain aspects of the collage. For example, when the door is closed, a handmade wooden frame highlights the peek-a-boo hole in its center. Fences made of pale wood in front of the side boxes serve to enclose the photos as well as to draw our eye to them.

6. Add thick "shingles" of decorative paper to the rooftops. Paint as desired, outlining the edges with metallic paint.

MATERIALS

- ⊙ foam core
- ⊙ rice paper
- ⊙ photocopies of photographs
- ⊙ various print materials such as maps, stamps, music paper
- ⊙ embellishments such as shells, buttons, beads, coins, keys, jewels
- ⊙ acrylic paints in various colors
- ⊙ metallic paints
- ⊙ adhesives: acrylic matte medium, textile glue, industrial-strength craft glue
- ⊙ basic collage supplies (see page 12)

⊙ **Carol Owen's Creativity Tips**

I take workshops and classes and go to seminars in all kinds of different media to keep ideas flowing. One of the most effective tools I've found comes from *The Artist's Way* by Julia Cameron—she calls it "filling the well." I keep binders of clippings of photographs, postcards, articles, and images that speak to me. Flipping through these books always stimulates my creativity.

❧ CLARA ❧

Composed of aged plaster, embossed wallpaper,
found objects, and a vintage photograph, this
multi-media collage has disguised itself as an
antique heirloom discovered in the attic. In it,
Paula Grasdal remembers what it was like to
play at her grandmother's house as a child. The
bottom drawer of her dresser was a treasure trove
of fascinating objects—old buttons, wooden
spools, and beads—a source of inspiration for
childhood artistry. Grasdal chose this photograph
of her grandmother at age five to create a link
between the generations and both of their
childhoods.

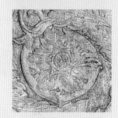

Dimensions: 11³/₄" × 14" (29¹/₂ cm × 36 cm) | Artist: Paula Grasdal

CLARA ⊚

1. Using diluted craft glue, attach wallpaper and the plaster-coated canvas to a plywood board and roll with a brayer to flatten out air bubbles. Paint the wallpaper with metallic acrylics, wiping away excess paint on the raised areas while still wet. Layer a wash of diluted burnt-umber acrylic paint over the wallpaper and the plaster to create an aged effect. When dry, lightly sand the painted plaster and wipe with diluted yellow-ochre paint.

2. Mount the photograph or color photocopy onto heavy paper with acrylic medium and roll with a brayer. Create a frame out of plaster-coated cheese-cloth and adhere onto the photocopy with craft glue (as a variation, incorporate copies of old letters in the frame). Attach the assembled piece to the painted plaster background with more craft glue.

3. Dab leaf sizing on the frame in a random fashion. Apply the copper leaf with your fingers, using a soft artist's brush to clear away excess (save fragments for other projects). Let dry, and then lightly sand for a distressed finish.

4. Further embellish the collage with found objects that reflect the character of the person in your collage; adhere them with the industrial-strength glue. Apply botanical fragments and fabric scraps with a little acrylic medium.

MATERIALS

- ⊚ piece of plywood (in desired size)
- ⊚ plaster-coated canvas
- ⊚ plaster-coated cheesecloth
- ⊚ strip of embossed wallpaper
- ⊚ heavy paper
- ⊚ vintage photograph or color photocopy
- ⊚ embellishments such as fern fragments, fabric scraps, old buttons
- ⊚ acrylic paints
- ⊚ imitation copper leaf
- ⊚ adhesives: acrylic gel medium, craft glue, leaf sizing, industrial-strength craft glue
- ⊚ basic collage supplies (see page 12)

⊚ Paula Grasdal's Creativity Tips

Surrounding myself with an abundance of found objects and art materials as I work inspires my creative process. Easily reached and visible supplies have a subliminal influence on my artwork; unexpected elements spontaneously find their way into a project, introducing a playful approach. Using what is available in my studio also creates a framework or arena for experimentation, which is invaluable when getting started.

❦❦ MEMORY OF HOME ❦❦
FROM AN ISLAND

*Candace Walters created this memory painting
with collage elements as an exploration of life's
process. The egg image represents our beginnings,
the portrait of the artist's daughter is the
culmination. In between, there are journeys we
take in sleeping, dreaming, and wakefulness.
Walters playfully collaged images of animals
onto the painting in clusters, almost like thoughts
or memories gathered around her daughter's
head. The animals are speaking to each other
in dialogue bubbles, allowing us to see into the
fantasy life of the daughter as imagined by
the artist.*

Dimensions: 32" × 22" (81 cm × 56 cm) | Artist: Candace Walters

STEPS

1. Begin with a strong, heavy paper and set up your work area so your materials are close at hand. Try starting with a wash of a color to eliminate the "shock" and fear of the white paper. Consider a variety of techniques—such as working with a rag or spackling trowel—so that the beginning surface is surprising.

2. Collage found papers onto select areas of the background, then draw and paint images freely, trying not to become specific too quickly. Allow the piece to evolve. Let your ideas and images ebb and flow, disappearing and re-emerging just as memories do. Enjoy the mystery of this process. This piece seems to float between the various images it contains: the painted egg, the collaged talking animals, and the portrait.

3. Working intuitively, build up the piece with more collage materials. Sand back to what's beneath to reveal things; this can be surprising and adds to the visual process of "remembering." The artist refers to this process of adding and taking away elements as the "kitchen sink" method: Throw it all in and then eliminate the clutter to reveal what is rich, provoking, and telling.

MATERIALS

- ☉ pencils
- ☉ pastels
- ☉ watercolors
- ☉ gouache
- ☉ assorted found papers including wallpaper (for the clothing) and pages from old books
- ☉ steel wool
- ☉ adhesive: acrylic matte or gloss medium
- ☉ basic collage supplies (see page 12)

☉ Candace Walters's Creativity Tips

Take a day and visit favorite sources of inspiration—bookstores, flea markets, old photos and scrapbooks, old letters—and enjoy the hunt for materials. A day of this is bound to open up the dreaded block, or what I refer to as "not having an idea in my head." Try out all sorts of experimental techniques as a way of reinventing and re-energizing your creativity. I have even advised my students to run over their work with their car to drastically alter the surface—the result could be dreadful, but it might end up being something remarkable.

TRANSFORMING PAPER FOR COLLAGE

PAULA GRASDAL

Decorating or altering paper for collage can add atmosphere and character to your projects. Creating your own collage materials opens up a vast array of techniques to experiment with and can be a good way to "get in the mood" to make an artwork. Playing with colors, textures, and materials encourages ideas and inspiration to flow.

PAINT EFFECTS

There are many ways to create painted textures on paper for use in collage. Applying paints or inks with objects other than a brush yields an infinite variety of results. Here are a few ideas to get you started. To create depth: Dip a sea sponge in paint and dab it onto paper in layers, starting with the darkest color and finishing with the lightest. For various mottled effects: Use newsprint to lift wet paint off of painted paper; coat crumpled plastic wrap with a thin layer of paint and stamp onto paper; or paint a variety of colors onto freezer paper, fold it in half to blend the colors, peel apart, and press onto paper.

Monoprinting also produces interesting textures or imagery and can be done without a printmaking press (see pages 184, 187, and 240). Brush or roll water-soluble paints or printing inks onto a printing plate made of Mylar film, place it paint-side down onto absorbent paper, and burnish the back of the plate with a wooden spoon to transfer the design. Other techniques: Before printing, draw into the painted printing plate with a dry brush, press textures into the paint, or wipe off areas with a rag.

MAKING TEXTURES WITH FOUND OBJECTS

Create unique papers for collage using found objects from nature or around the house. For a batik effect: Place paper over a textured object and rub it with a wax crayon or oil pastel, then brush a wash of water-based paint over the rubbing. Stamp designs using found objects such as a string-wrapped block, bubble wrap, doilies, leaves or any other textured item that looks promising. Found objects can also serve as stencils to block out areas of paint and create a negative shape.

ANTIQUING

Many of the collage artists in this book use antiquing techniques to evoke the past. Look at old decaying surfaces for inspiration and try some of the following ideas to achieve a patina of age in your work. Coat heavy paper with plaster, bend it when dry to create cracks, then add a wash of paint. Spread modeling paste or spackling on paper and stamp textures or motifs into the wet surface. Paint gesso onto craft tissue, let dry, then stain with liquid acrylics or inks. Add dry pigments to clear polishing wax and rub it onto painted papers. Tear, sand, or peel papers after they have been glued in place. Brush varnish or crackle glazes over painted paper or images. Crumple paper and spray it with diluted paint to emphasize the wrinkles (brown paper bags work well). This is just a sampling of ways to create striking effects on paper. For more inspiration, see page 271 for suggested reading.

❧ GALLERY OF ❧ INSPIRATION

Dimensions: 32" × 22" (81 cm × 56 cm) | Artist: Candace Walters

MEMORY VESSEL

Candace Walters created this richly textured painting with collage using a process common to much of her work: painting, layering, and unearthing. Working in many layers (using wallpapers, antique handwritten letters, and vintage receipts), she created intuitively, exploring themes related to female mysticism and memory. She then scraped at the surface to reveal images and meanings hidden below. Clear images—the portrait of her daughter gazing at something the viewer cannot see, an egg and its shadow, a shell—are surrounded by a misty veil of color, texture, and partial imagery, creating an impression of memories lingering at the edges of consciousness.

Dimensions: 11" × 8" (28 cm x 20 cm) | Artist: Nina Bagley

BOOK OF TREES

Using diverse found materials, Nina Bagley created a complex accordion-fold artist book inspired by memories of her Southern childhood, when trees were guardians and friends. The base is covered with antique optical testing lenses sandwiched over old photographs of trees. Attached to the base by vintage jewelry parts are six intricately decorated metal panels and a top panel of embossed leather, made from the cover of a Victorian photo album. A treasure trove of findings, Bagley's book is characterized as much by what is hidden as what is visible: a poem tucked into a transparent glassine envelope; a man's face just visible behind metal doors; words etched and pasted onto the backs of things.

BALANCED HEAD

For this hanging assemblage mounted on a wooden cigar box lid, Janet Hofacker was inspired by the combination of the doll's head and wooden exercise tool (they seemed to "just fit together nicely"). By juxtaposing delicate porcelain with a rusted metal plate, she reveals and emphasizes the nature of each. The lightness of the porcelain doll head, tentatively balanced on its wooden wheels, makes a playful statement against the more serious, industrial character of the rusted metal backdrop and heavy spike frame. Glass marbles and pieces of a cut-up collage add visual interest and a further sense of whimsy.

Dimensions: 9" × 10" (23 cm × 25 cm) | Artist: Janet Hofacker

Dimensions: 10" × 6" (25 cm × 15 cm) | Artist: Judi Riesch

ALTERED FACES

Judi Riesch transformed an old wooden address book she found at an antiques shop into this multi-media artwork. She substituted vintage photographs for the existing pages, and reinforced the holes with metal washers. Using acrylic paint, gel medium, pencils, vintage papers, tintypes, wire mesh, buttons, and beeswax, she collaged directly onto the portraits. Riesch prefers to work with actual vintage photographs rather than photocopies because, with their genuine faces captured in time, they provide an intimate connection with the past. Intriguingly, the faces in her book are altered or obscured: Some eyes are blacked out, others peer through wire mesh, and still others look outward with an unfettered gaze.

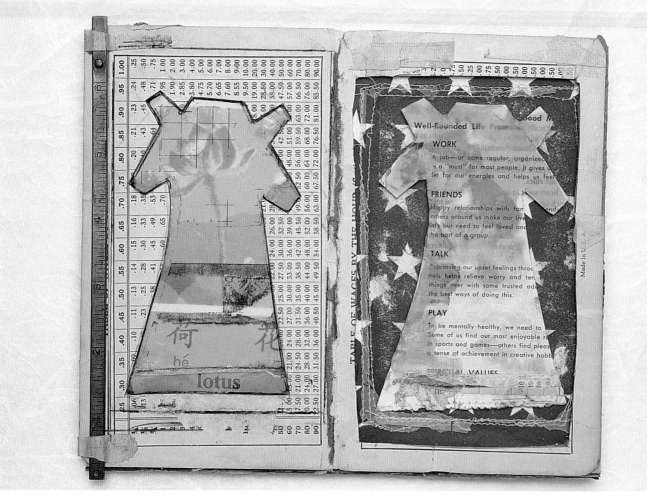

Dimensions: 6 ½" × 8" (17 cm × 20 cm) | Artist: Jane Maxwell

MEASURING-UP

A vintage ledger book, old metal ruler, translucent vellum, and inspiration from doll cutouts are the essential elements in Jane Maxwell's expressive piece about feminine identity. A simple dress form recalls the cutout paper dolls so many women played with as children. Here the meaning is more complex, representing prefab roles shaped by social expectations of how women should act and look. Yet in the details—a lotus blossom struggling to be seen, random drippings of candle wax—Maxwell seems to offer hope that we can shape these forms to suit ourselves.

Dimensions: 7 ½" × 9" (19 cm × 23 cm) | Artist: Emily Trespas

UNTITLED

The subtle color shifts of this piece belie the many processes and layers Emily Trespas used in its composition: To over-printed layers of transparent monoprints she added chine collé elements and a collaged funnel shape. Inspired by frescoes of the "Life of Saint Francis," in Italy, where she saw what looked like a birdcage with funnel shapes floating around it, the artist created a series of mixed-media mono-prints based on these images. There is a surrealistic discon-nect between the funnel, with its evocation of medicine and measuring, and the birdcage, which speaks of nature and also containment. Here, the funnel shapes exist outside the cage almost like the souls of St. Francis's birds, fluttering between earth and heaven.

I'LL GO THERE

Constructed with maps from different countries, the artist's travel photos, and posters of Hindu gods and flowers, Chantale Légaré's mixed-media collage asks us to look at where we are going. She began with a small painting of feet decorated with *mendhi* patterns to symbolize celebrations. Roads sprout out of the feet and lead to two perfect lotus blooms. Map fragments are juxtaposed with the cells of the body to represent sense memories of places and the images, colors, sounds, and scents associated with them. The brilliantly colored landscape is dominated by the lotuses, which symbolize the ultimate path.

Dimensions: 20" × 15" (51 cm × 38 cm) | Artist: Chantale Légaré

LOTUS

Working with ink and acrylics on a wallpaper canvas, Stanford Kay created a piece in which a flower sprouts roots reminiscent of the human respiratory system. Using Chinoiserie landscape scenes as a background, he added two collage elements: a color photocopy of a pink lotus blossom, the Asian symbol of enlightenment, and photocopied medieval drawings of buildings placed along the bottom edge. The collaged village puts the floating organ-and-lotus image in context as elevated, much like medieval engravings of botanical studies would float their subjects over a landscape. The artist plays with scale and imagery to create a mysterious world where diverse cultural references converge.

Dimensions: 18" × 24" (46 cm × 61 cm) | Artist: Stanford Kay

Dimensions: 26" × 28" (66 cm × 71 cm) | Artist: Tracy Spadafora

BULB GARDEN

This piece, encaustic and collage on braced plywood, is based on a sculpture previously made by the artist. She had painted leaf skeletons onto chandelier bulbs and dipped them in beeswax before placing them in a black iron pot filled with pebbles. Working from memory to make this painting, Tracy Spadafora took texts from encyclopedias, novels, and a repeated black-and-white image of a swing and buried them between layers of encaustic paint. The lightbulbs popping out of the pot look like floral bulbs while scales in the background symbolize the fragile equilibrium between humanity and nature.

Dimensions: Six 4" h × 4" w × 1" d (10 cm × 10 cm × 3 cm) boxes | Artist: Deborah Putnoi

From left (top row): EYESIGHT, ELECTRICITY, END;
(bottom): RESPIRATION, NEW TIME, ATROCITIES

The collaged boxes in this group are part of a larger series by Deborah Putnoi in which each collage explores a question and juxtaposing them creates a dialog among the disparate elements. For each box, she used a wide variety of materials: pieces of embroidered cloth, canvas with painted text, metal plates scratched with images, scraps of drawings, and colorful paints. The central images—eyes, electric cords and plugs, people's lungs, animals, portraits, pieces of text—resonate in context to raise questions about how we see, the impulses that connect us, our relationship to plants (through breath) and animals, and how we communicate.

Composition XVI   Marianne Fisker Pierce

Dimensions: 24½" × 18½" (62 cm × 47 cm) | Artist: Marianne Fisker Pierce

COMPOSITION XVI

To explore her ongoing fascination with humanmade forms found in construction machinery and road markings, Marianne Fisker Pierce took a series of photos of the "Big Dig" in Boston, Massachusetts, a particularly complex and dramatic construction project. First, she took endless shots of the machinery and detritus at the site. The rest of the process involved choosing from among the 4" by 6" (10 cm × 15 cm) prints (some of them duplicates), laying them out loosely on a table, and then shuffling and rearranging them until a composition emerged. The result: a quilt-like piece dominated by reds and blacks, held together by the tensions created by intersecting lines and juxtaposed forms.

Dimensions: 19 ½" × 19" (48 cm × 50 cm) | Artist: Tracy Spadafora

UNTITLED

In dream analysis, the image of the house represents the soul or self, as it also does in the work of Tracy Spadafora. She made this monotype with collage using thin layers of etching ink, pieces of maps (in color), and black-and-white aerial photographs of large cities, all of which she applied in layers with an etching press. Through the juxtaposition of these various images, she raises questions about public and private space by positing the role of the individual (house) against the societal demands of an already large world (city) that continues to expand and grow.

Dimensions: 19" × 24" (48 cm × 61 cm) | Artist: Cynthia Winika

SWIMMING I

Cynthia Winika created this evocative collage using encaustic and oil paints, photocopied images from old books, and the technique of scribing a handwritten text into the translucent wax, smearing it with oil color, and then wiping for a drypoint, multilayered effect. The artist likens being under the sea to a dream state, possibly one of mourning. The fish leaping up are emerging from the dream, and the boat represents survival and safety.

THE EARTH ANGEL: PORCH IN SUMMER

Inspired by memories of studying the summer night sky as a child, Amy Kitchin built an assemblage out of a wooden cigar box, foam core, acrylic paints, and natural objects that explores the complex relationships between the smallest natural forms and the vastness of the universe. Juxtaposing seedpods, twigs, and images of dragonflies against painted constellations, she posits the idea that even as we sleep, the universe expands and nature continues to regenerate.

Dimensions: 13" h × 9" w × 2" d (33 cm × 23 cm × 5 cm) | Artist: Amy Kitchin

RELIC IV

In this multi-media fabric collage, Paula Grasdal pays homage to the Cabinets of Curiosity of seventeenth-century Europe: small, personalized museums created by enthusiastic collectors seeking to make sense of the world and its marvels. Typically these cabinets were filled with wondrous artifacts from nature, science, and culture. The colorful piece includes images of fossils, a butterfly, and astronomical instruments, as well as an attached vial of sparkling pyrite. Grasdal used numerous techniques such as photo transfer, appliqué, and machine embroidery to create a richly textured and layered effect.

Dimensions: 17 ½" × 14 ½" (44 cm × 37 cm) | Artist: Paula Grasdal

PRAYER 1

This mixed-media collage, made with gesso, acrylic paint, and watercolor crayons, is part of Karen Michel's continuing Prayer series, which deals with humanity's fundamental dreams and wishes. This particular work has been composed of essential symbols: home, a place of shelter and sanctuary; the hand, or creativity; the moon and ocean for humanity's connection to nature; a lotus, offering hope for enlightenment; the heart, the conduit of love and compassion; and a solitary cell, the artist's reminder that we are one among many.

Dimensions: 26" × 14" (66 cm × 36 cm) | Artist: Karen Michel
From the collection of the Mihale Family

Dimensions: 5 ½" × 7 ¼" (14 cm × 18 ½ cm) | Artist: Emily Trespas

UNTITLED

The pages shown are from an artist's book created by Emily Trespas while she was living and working in Rome. Walking the streets of the city, she gathered bits of paper and labels, peeled flyers from walls, and plucked wrappers from fruit. She frequented the flea market for old photographs to accompany found passport photos. She collaged these artifacts into the book, combining them with colorful painted and drawn passages. A journal such as this can be a wonderful reminder of a trip or serve as inspiration for future art projects.

Dimensions: 14" ×11" (36 cm × 28 cm) | Artist: Laurinda T. Bedingfield

SEASON'S END

In this memory collage, made of Polaroid transfers, handmade paper, gold leaf, and acrylic paints on canvas, Laurinda T. Bedingfield looks at death, change, connection, and spring's promise of rebirth through memories of her grandfather. She printed old slides as Polaroid transfers, which gives the images a timeworn, nostalgic quality. The photos record his annual ritual of burying the family's fig trees to protect them from the New England winter and unearthing them again in the spring. One photo shows him digging, another resting. Bedingfield further personalized the piece by incorporating organic material from her backyard, a piece of twine, and a handwritten text.

Dimensions: 9" h × 11" w × 9" d (23 cm × 28 cm × 23 cm) | Artist: Aparna Agrawal

ONE THREAD

Aparna Agrawal created this translucent and delicate sculpture using the simplest of materials: paper, thread, and wax. The organic shape is reminiscent of forms found in nature such as seedpods or egg sacks. Once she had shaped and sewn the paper into a standing tent-like structure, she collaged small rice paper shirts onto the inside surface, connecting them to each other by a single thread. In this way, she relays a vision of the world in which people are individual yet tethered together, belonging to a larger humanity. However, the structure is fragile, the thread is fragile, and so, ultimately, is the connection.

Dimensions: 13" × 10" (33 cm × 25 cm) | Artist: Carol Owen

TIME REMEMBERED

Leaving room for people to invent their own narratives is key to the work of Carol Owen and this piece is a prime example. On a base of foam core covered in rice paper, she created a colorful shrine with washes of paint and embellishments such as vintage valentines and postcards, bits of lace and jewelry, and photocopies of old photographs. The heavily collaged and layered piece, with its haunting black-and-white images, offers tantalizing glimpses of past memories and half-told stories, whose completion depends on the imagination of the viewer.

Dimensions: 24" × 32" (61 cm × 81 cm) | Artist: Rosemary Broton Boyle

UNTITLED

Rosemary Broton Boyle explores the themes of love and romance in this mixed-media collage, composed using layers of various papers, washes of acrylic paints and crackling glazes, and photo transfer techniques. The two deer symbolize a couple settling into the comfort of loving and being loved. Vintage ledger papers collaged on the surface represent love letters and communication while decorative elements such as the leafy embossed wallpaper and translucent rice paper add a romantic Victorian feel.

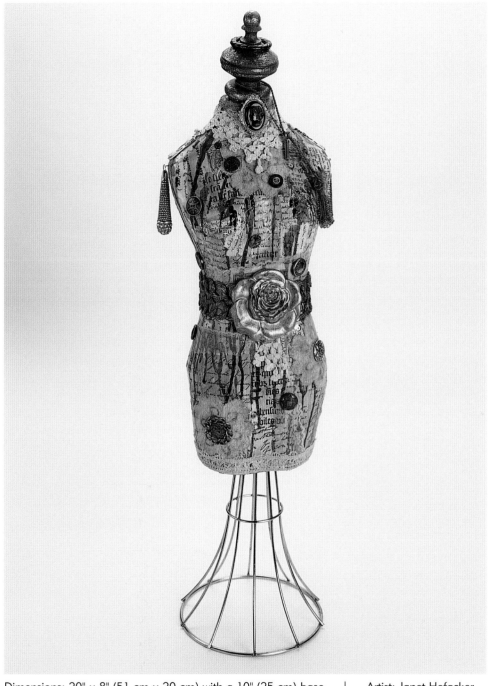

RENAISSANCE ARMOR

For this assemblage, a papier-mâché dress form collaged with paper and found objects, Janet Hofacker sought to use seemingly useless objects to make a work of art. To create depth, she worked in layers, beginning with torn pieces of parchment paper, followed by tissue paper and sections of lace. Once this first layer was dry, she painted the form using a sea sponge and three shades of diluted acrylic paint. After adding gold-leaf highlights, she let her imagination run wild, gluing on myriad embellishments: tassels, buttons, sequins, junk jewelry, rhinestones, and finials.

Dimensions: 20" × 8" (51 cm × 20 cm) with a 10" (25 cm) base | Artist: Janet Hofacker

BOOKS WILL GET YOU STARTED

Making imaginative use of found objects, foam core, and a photocopy machine, Lynne Perrella reinvented a Victorian birdcage as a playful home for a paper theater. First she repaired the cage and cleaned it up with paint. Then she mounted archival prints of theaters, players, and antique books onto foam core to create the sets and actors, building another platform within the cage so she could house two theaters. The artist has created an atmospheric miniature world that celebrates the history of the English language.

Dimensions: 36" h × 24" w × 10" d (91 cm × 61 cm × 25 cm) | Artist: Lynne Perrella

Dimensions: 46" × 34" (117 cm × 86 cm) | Artist: Mark Schofield

ON THE BOARDS

Mark Schofield's multi-media assemblage is a whimsical homage to the fantastical eclecticism of the performing arts. Drawing on a wide range of images from dance, performance art, Asian puppetry, poetry slams, and film, the piece is an international stage set with something for everyone to see. Because of its complex layering, Schofield composed the entire piece before gluing. As a final step, he integrated diverse elements—among them moldings, marquee letters, a brass horn, scrap metal, a cardboard jester, a mask, linoleum scraps, various photocopies, an audio-tape reel, and three pennies—using colored pencils, inks, and acrylic paints.

BABYBOX DELUXE

Olivia Thomas transformed a feeling of being overwhelmed into this fun art piece made of a round gift box covered in recycled fabric that she stamped and painted. To this she added a doll's head surrounded by a chaotic heaping of found objects—Monopoly game pieces, dice, seashells, a compass, buttons, holeless beads and pearls, and plastic toys. To represent the many hands reaching out for her, she glued doll's hands to the bottom of the box to act as "feet."

Dimensions: 9" (23 cm) tall | Artist: Olivia Thomas

OLD-FASHIONED ROMANCE

Kathy Cano-Murillo created a shrine to all things romantic by mounting vintage Hollywood images and crinkly pieces of tin into a shallow cigar box and garnishing it with loads of rhinestones, paper and fabric roses, glitter, and a lush frame of greenery. Her inspiration: the lustful glances, tender kisses, budding roses, and flaming hearts of vintage Technicolor popcorn flicks.

Dimensions: 15" h × 8" w × 2" d (38 cm × 20 cm × 5 cm)　|　Artist: Kathy Cano-Murillo

DIRECTORY OF ARTISTS

APARNA AGRAWAL
16 Crescent Street
Cambridge, MA 02138 USA
aparnaku@attbi.com
www.aparnaart.com
254

CAROL ANDREWS
232½ North Fillmore Street
Arlington, VA 22201-1228 USA
74, 75

DEBRA L. ARTER
HC 64, Box 183
South Bristol, ME 14568 USA
83, 102, 103

NINA BAGLEY
796 Savannah Drive
Sylva, NC 28779 USA
papernina@aol.com
www.ninabagleydesign.com
236–237

ANN BALDWIN
San Rafael, CA USA
art@annbaldwin.com
www.annbaldwin.com
221–223

LAURINDA T. BEDINGFIELD
61 Putnam Street
Somerville, MA 02143 USA
617-591-8192
pdog@110.net
253

FELICIA BELAIR-RIGDON
105 No. Union Street
Alexandria, VA 22314 USA
41

DOUGLAS BELL
97 Walk Hill Street
Jamaica Plain, MA 02130 USA
617-522-7068
116, 118–123, 130, 136

JENNIFER M. BERRINGER
9300 Pine View Lane
Clinton, MD 20735 USA
78, 88–93, 104, 136

ROSEMARY BROTON BOYLE
Artists West Association
144 Moody Street
Waltham, MA 02459 USA
Phone: (781) 736-0299
256

MERYL BRATER
101 Franklin Street
Allston, MA 02134 USA
87, 102

KATHY CANO-MURILLO
4223 W. Orchid Lane
Phoenix, AZ 85051 USA
kathymurillo@hotmail.com
www.kathycanomurillo.com
193–195, 261

GORDON CARLISLE
P. O. Box 464
855 Islington Street
Portsmouth, NH 03802-0464 USA
16, 42

ERIKA CARTER
2440 Killarney Way SE
Bellevue, WA 98004 USA
72

ROBIN M. CHANDLER
Fulbright Scholar/SIS
University of Witwaters Rand
Parktown Village
P.O. Wits 2050
Parktown 2193
Republic of South Africa
25, 44

CHANTALE LÉGARÉ
RR 2 Box 999
Vineyard Haven, MA 02568 USA
508-696-3007
chalegare@earthlink.com
151–153, 242

PETER MADDEN
109 F Street
Boston, MA 02127 USA
113, 135

JANE MAXWELL
Newton, MA USA
janemaxwell@attbi.com
163–165, 240

THERESE MAY
651 North 4th Street
San Jose, CA 95112 USA
49, 71

KAREN L. MCCARTHY
141 Warren Street
Arlington, MA 02174 USA
32–39, 42, 138

KAREN MICHEL
kmichelny@hotmail.com
www.karenmichel.com
209–211, 251

DIANE MILLER
261 Garfield Place
Brooklyn, NY 11215 USA
100, 101

BARBARA J. MORTENSON
633 Stetson Road
Elkins Park, PA 19027 USA
72, 73

EMILY MYEROW
Fine Design Art Studio
Saxonville Studios
1602 B. Concord Street
Framingham, MA 01701 USA
82, 100

DOMINIE NASH
Bethesda, MD USA
48, 70, 71

GINA OCHIOGROSSO
930 Morgan Avenue
Schenectady, NY 12309 USA
40

HELEN PIEROTTI ORTH
Collage Mystique
2045 Broadway
San Francisco, CA 94115 USA
14

CAROL OWEN
Fearrington Post 54
Pittsboro, NC 27312 USA
919-542-0616
gowen1@nc.rr.com
224–226, 255

RACHEL PAXTON
P. O. Box 2129
Jamaica Plain, MA 02130 USA
617-427-1065
21, 26–31, 43, 138

LYNNE PERRELLA
54 Jennifer Lane
Ancram, NY 12502 USA
www.LKPerrella.com
181–183, 258

LINDA S. PERRY
Art Quilts
96 Burlington Street
Lexington, MA 02173 USA
46, 56, 70

MARIANNE FISKER PIERCE
16 Trotting Horse Drive
Lexington, MA 02173 USA
781-862-0640
246

DEBORAH PUTNOI
Belmont, MA USA
artforachange@aol.com
79, 94–99, 105, 139, 154–157, 245

JUDI RIESCH
4716 Northside Drive, NW
Atlanta, GA 30327 USA
404-250-1336
jjriesch@aol.com
www.itsmysite.com/judiriesch
145–147, 239

NANCY RUBENS
340 West 72nd Street
New York, NY 10023 USA
109, 130

SANDRA SALAMONY
80 Chestnut Street
Cambridge, MA 02139 USA
sandranoel@aol.com
203–205

MARK SCHOFIELD
Mark Schofield Illustration
102 First Avenue S., #321-B
Seattle, WA 98134 USA
206-623-9539
Represented by Sharon Dodge
800-ARTSTOCK or 206-282-3672
www.illustrationworks.com
259

ELOISE PICKARD SMITH
Contact Eloise Pickard Smith Gallery
Cowell College
University of California
Santa Cruz, CA 95064 USA
408-459-2953
20, 21, 40

DAWN SOUTHWORTH
63 Bennett Street
Gloucester, MA 01930 USA
135

TRACY SPADAFORA
Somerville, MA USA
spad4@earthlink.net
www.vernonstreet.com
244, 247

OLIVIA THOMAS
15441 N. First Street
Phoenix, AZ 85022 USA
602-993-3246
PEZMAN@concentric.net
178–180, 260

EMILY TRESPAS
180 Main Street
Andover, MA 01810 USA
241, 252

NANCY VIRBILA
41 Alpine Trail
Sparta, NJ 07871-1508 USA
43

CLARA WAINWRIGHT
57 Upland Road
Brookline, MA 02146 USA
617-628-0060
11, 53, 57, 58–63, 75, 139

CANDACE WALTERS
c/o Clark Gallery
145 Lincoln Road
Lincoln, MA 01773 USA
781-259-8303
230–232, 235

LORI A. WARNER
33 Soley Street
Charlestown, MA 02129 USA
132

ELLEN WINEBERG
Kendall Center for the Arts
226 Beech Street
Belmont, MA 02178 USA
10, 112, 117, 132

CYNTHIA WINIKA
87 Hasbrouck Road
New Paltz, NY 12561 USA
845-255-9338
248

JOYCE A. YESUCEVITZ
204 Endicott Street
Boston, MA 02113 USA
134

RESOURCES

This guide is organized by project and by vendor. Look under the project name to find out about the particular products and materials used, then consult the vendor listing below.

EXPLORING CREATIVITY

page 148, Temple

Papermaking pulps, felts, and cotton linters are available through Dick Blick Art Materials and at art supply stores.

Sobo Premium Craft & Textile Glue is available at craft stores.

Methyl cellulose is available at Utrecht and other art supply stores.

page 151, Crossings

Lauan is available at the Home Depot and lumber stores.

Glass-etching solution is available at craft stores and at Pearl Paint.

CHRONICLING RELATIONSHIPS

page 160, Pond Life

Encaustic paints and heated palettes are available at R&F Handmade Paints.

page 172, Le Mariage

Handmade paper is available at Twinrocker and art supply stores.

EXPRESSING DREAMS AND WISHES

page 181, Ceremonial Figure I

Encaustic paints and heated palettes are available at R&F Handmade Paints.

Arches 88 printmaking paper is available at art supply stores.

Lauan (see Glossary, page 13) is available at the Home Depot and lumber stores.

page 184, Transformation

Rice papers are available at Rugg Road and art supply stores.

page 187, Arcadia

BFK Rives and Arches 88 printmaking paper are available at art supply stores.

Rice papers are available at Rugg Road and art supply stores.

INSPIRED BY NATURE

page 200, Secret Garden

BFK Rives heavyweight paper is available at art supply stores.

page 203, Shhh…

Moss green glaze by Plaid and dry metallic pigment in Sunset Gold are manufactured by Pearl Ex. Available at art supply stores.

Brass-darkening solution is available at woodworking supply stores or wherever furniture restoration supplies are sold.

Hardware cloth is available at hardware stores.

page 209, Urban Birdsong

Portfolio Series water-soluble oil pastels are manufactured by Crayola.

page 212, Lilies of the Valley

Sobo Premium Craft & Textile Glue is available at craft stores.

CREATING VISUAL MEMOIRS

page 221, The Way We Were

Acrylic matte medium, heavy gel medium, fluid acrylics (in Transparent Yellow Oxide, Quinacridone Crimson, Paynes Gray, and Titan Buff), and tube paint in Deep Gold are all manufactured by Golden. Available at art supply stores.

Acid-free paper used for printing out scanned images: Strathmore Professional Artist Ink Jet Paper (medium surface). Strathmore Artist Papers are available at art supply stores.

page 230, Memory of Home From an Island

Golden matte and gloss medium is available at art supply stores.

For information on the products listed as well as other craft materials, contact:

A.C. MOORE CRAFT STORES

See www.acmoore.com *for store locations*

art and crafts supplies

THE ART STORE

401 Park Drive

Boston, MA 02215 USA

617-247-3322

art supplies and handmade papers

DICK BLICK ART MATERIALS

800-723-2787

See www.dickblick.com

HOME DEPOT

See www.homedepot.com *for store locations*

PEARL PAINT COMPANY

308 Canal Street

New York, NY 10013 USA

800-451-PEARL for catalog

art and crafts supplies

PORTFOLIO SERIES WATER-SOLUBLE OIL PASTELS

See www.portfolioseries.com *or* www.crayola.com

R&F HANDMADE PAINTS

506 Broadway

Kingston, NY 12401 USA

800-206-8088

See also www.rfpaints.com

RUGG ROAD PAPER COMPANY

105 Charles Street

Boston, MA 02114 USA

617-742-0002

handmade specialty papers

STRATHMORE ARTIST PAPERS

See www.strathmoreartist.com *for suppliers*

TWINROCKER HANDMADE PAPER

100 East Third Street

P.O. Box 413

Brookston, IN 47923 USA

800-757-8946

twinrocker@twinrocker.com

UTRECHT ART

800-223-9132

See www.utrechtart.com for store locations or to order online

art supplies

INTERNATIONAL RESOURCES

CREATIVE CRAFTS

11 The Square

Winchester

Hampshire SO23 9ES UK

+44 01962-856266

www.creativecrafts.co.uk

HOBBYCRAFT

Head Office

Bournemouth, UK

+44 1202-596-100

stores throughout the UK

JOHN LEWIS

Flagship Store

Oxford Street

London W1A 1EX

+44 207-629-7711

www.johnlewis.co.uk

stores throughout the UK

ECKERSLEY'S ARTS, CRAFTS, AND IMAGINATION

+61 1-300-657-766 for catalog

www.eckersleys.com.au

store locations in New South Wales, Queensland, South Australia, and Victoria, Australia

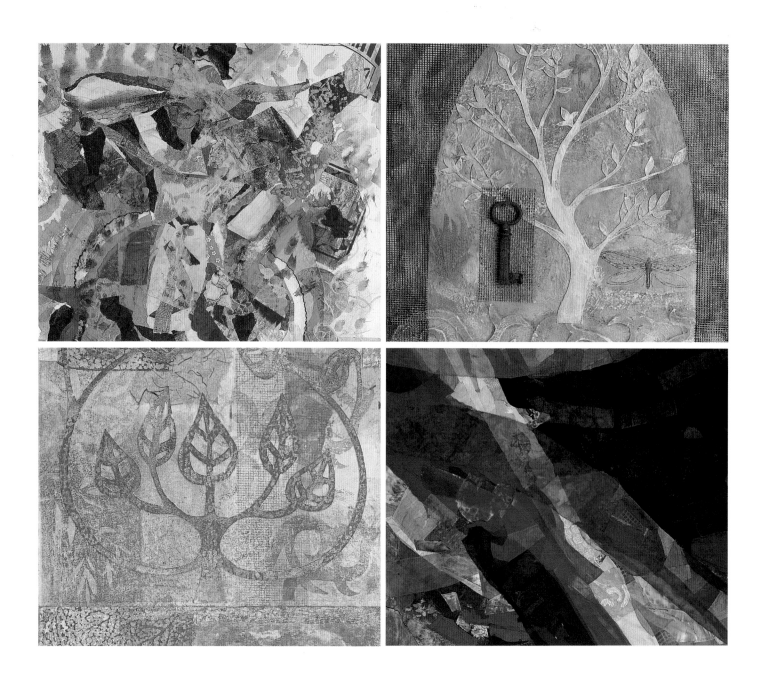

BIBLIOGRAPHY

Ades, Dawn. *Photomontage*. New York: Thames and Hudson, 1976.

Bronner, Gerald F. *The Art of Collage*. Worcester, MA: Davis Publications, 1978.

Bruce-Mitford, Miranda. *The Illustrated Book of Signs and Symbols*. London: Dorling Kindersley, 1996.

Caws, Mary Ann, ed. Joseph Cornell's *Theatre of the Mind: Selected Diaries, Letters, and Files*. New York: Thames and Hudson, 1993.

Digby, Joan and John. *The Collage Handbook*. London: Thames and Hudson, 1985.

Fontana, David. *The Secret Language of Symbols*. San Francisco: Chronicle Books, 1993.

Goldsworthy, Andy. *A Collaboration with Nature*. New York: Henry N. Abrams, 1990.

Guiley, Rosemary Ellen. *The Encyclopedia of Dreams: Symbols and Interpretations*. New York: Crossroads, 1993.

Harlow, William M. *Art Forms from Plant Life*. New York: Dover Publications, 1966, 1976.

Hoffman, Katherine, ed. *Collage: Critical Views*. New York: State University of New York at Stony Brook, 1989.

Larbalestier, Simon. *The Art and Craft of Collage*. San Francisco: Chronicle Books, 1995.

Leland, Nita and Virginia Lee Williams. *Creative Collage Techniques*. Cincinnati: North Light Books, 1994.

Mattera, Joanne. *The Art of Encaustic Painting: Contemporary Expression in the Ancient Medium of Pigmented Wax*. New York: Watson-Guptill Publications, 2001.

McNiff, Shaun. *Trust the Process: An Artist's Guide to Letting Go*. Boston: Shambhala Publications, 1998.

Romano, Clare, and John and Tim Ross. *The Complete Printmaker*. New York: The Free Press, 1990.

Rothamel, Susan Pickering. *The Art of Paper Collage*. New York: Sterling Publishing Company, 2001.

Smith, Barbara Lee. *Celebrating the Stitch: Contemporary Embroidery of North America*. Newtown, CT: The Taunton Press, 1991.

Turner, Silvie. *Which Paper?* New York: Design Press, 1991.

Waldman, Diane. *Collage, Assemblage, and the Found Object*. New York: Harry N. Abrams, 1992.

Welch, Nancy. *Creative Paper Art: Techniques for Transforming the Surface*. New York: Sterling Publishing Company, 1999.

Wolfram, Eddie. *History of Collage*. New York: Macmillan Publishing Company, 1975.

Wright, Michael. *An Introduction to Mixed Media*. Scarborough, Ontario: Prentice Hall Canada, 1995.

RECOMMENDED READING

Atkinson, Jennifer L. *Collage Art: A Step-by-Step Guide and Showcase*. Gloucester, MA: Rockport Publishers, 1996.

Ayres, Julia. *Monotype: Mediums and Methods for Painterly Printmaking*. New York: Watson-Guptill Publications, 1991.

Cameron, Julia. *The Artist's Way: A Spiritual Path to Higher Creativity*. New York: G. P. Putnam's Sons, 1992.

Eichorn, Rosemary. *The Art of Fabric Collage: An Introduction to Creative Sewing*. Newtown, CT: The Taunton Press, 2000.

Frost, Seena B. *Soul Collage: An Intuitive Collage Process for Individuals and Groups*. Santa Cruz, CA: Hanford Mead Publishers, 2001.

Harrison, Holly and Paula Grasdal. *Collage for the Soul: Expressing Hopes and Dreams through Art*. Gloucester, MA: Rockport Publishers, 2003.

McRee, Livia. *Easy Transfers for Any Surface: Crafting with Images and Photos*. Gloucester, MA: Rockport Publishers, 2002.

Pearce, Amanda. *The Crafter's Complete Guide to Collage*. New York: Watson-Guptill, 1997.

ABOUT THE AUTHORS

Jennifer Atkinson received her M.A. in Art History from Boston University in 1983. She worked for a number of years at Clark Gallery, where she and her colleague Julie Bernson organized shows of found object and collage art. She has written book reviews for *Art New England*, a bimonthly publication, and has been appointed curator of the Fuller Museum of Art in Brockton, Massachusetts.

Holly Harrison is a freelance writer and editor. Her first craft book, *Angel Crafts: Graceful Gifts and Inspired Designs for 41 Projects*, was published by Rockport in April 2002. She has also contributed to numerous magazines, including *Metropolitan Home*. She and her husband recently moved to Concord, MA, where she finally has a room of her own for writing and crafting.

Paula Grasdal is a printmaker and mixed-media artist living in the Seattle area. She has contributed to several other Rockport publications, including *Angel Crafts: Graceful Gifts and Inspired Designs for 41 Projects*, *The Crafter's Project Book*, and *Making Shadow Boxes and Shrines*. Her work has been exhibited in galleries in the U.S. and Canada.